W9-CNI-430

A TASTE OF
TUSCANY

For Mama
with love.
Don't you wish
we were there?! Eating?!
♡ Mimi 10-19-93
no occasion. I just love you.

A TASTE OF
TUSCANY

John Dore Meis

PHOTOGRAPHS BY JOHN FERRO SIMS

Abbeville Press   Publishers
New York   London   Paris

For Paolo, Cara, Ludovico, Bernardo and Filippo,
my first, most endearing, and enduring taste of Tuscany

First published in the United States of America in 1993
by Abbeville Press, 488 Madison Avenue, New York NY10022

First published in Great Britain in 1993 by
PAVILION BOOKS LIMITED
26 Upper Ground, London SE1 9PD

Text copyright © John Dore Meis 1993
Photographs copyright © John Ferro Sims 1993

All rights reserved under international copyright conventions. No part of this book
may be reproduced or utilized in any form or by any means electronic or mechanical,
including photocopying, recording, or by any information storage and retrieval system,
without permission in writing from the publisher. Inquiries should be addressed to
Abbeville Publishing Group, 488 Madison Avenue, New York, NY 10022.
Printed and bound in Singapore.

Designed by Andrew Barron & Collins Clements Associates

A CIP catalogue record for this book is available from the British Library

ISBN 1-55859-466-3

The author and publisher are grateful for permission to use the recipe for Chestnut
Blossom Honey Ice Cream from *Chez Panisse Cooking* by Paul Bertolli with Alice Waters
published by Random House.

Page 1: Round-bellied demijohns of Chianti encased in traditional rush-work. *Page 2:* The
ancient hamlet of Villa a Sesta in the hills of Chianti not far from Siena. *Page 3:* A prickly
burr releases an autumnal harvest of chestnuts.

The author would like to thank Chester Aaron for constant
encouragement and constructive correction, Jennifer Grillo for her
help with interpreting, editing and translating the recipes, and Maria
Consolata Gerini for checking and double checking his Italian spelling.

The Romanesque abbey church of
Sant'Antimo near Montalcino,
Tuscany's most prestigious wine town.

CONTENTS

Introduction 8

———————— WINTER ————————

Harvesting and Pressing Olives for Oil 14
Sweets from Siena 22
Processing the Family Porker and Hunting for Wild Boar 30

———————— SPRING ————————

Edible Weeds, Spring Greens and Aromatic Vinegars 50
Sheep's Milk Cheese 62
Easter Chocolates and Paschal Lamb 70
A Nomadic Beekeeper and Monofloral Tree Honeys 78
Florentine Food 84

———————— SUMMER ————————

Villa Cooking Classes and a Baronial Banquet 100
A Feast of Fish on the Island of Elba 108
Alfresco Festivals 116

———————— AUTUMN ————————

Chestnut Gathering and Mushrooming near Lucca 130
Wine Making in Chianti 142
A Finale of White Truffles 150
Index 158

INTRODUCTION

I firmly believe the following: Italy is the most wonderful country in Europe; Tuscany is the most splendid region of Italy; Chianti is the most beautiful area in Tuscany and the section of Chianti where I live, the best place of all. As with all matters of faith, these beliefs are not subject to rational proof but it is just as well to know from the start the presuppositions upon which this book is based. They also explain why, even though I travel to many areas of Tuscany in these pages, from Lucca in the north to the island of Elba in the south, when given a choice I stay close to home.

I live above an old olive oil mill. Below my kitchen is an enormous room where huge granite stones weighing several tons have crushed olives for centuries. I sleep over the *orciaio*, the room where the *orci* are kept, splendid terracotta urns in which the olive oil is stored. There are a couple of *orci* in my garden. These, having developed cracks, are no longer suitable for holding oil. They are signed by the potter who made them and the oldest is dated 1692.

It is purely fortuitous, but fitting, that the structure which supports my daily life was built for producing olive oil. This green-gold liquid is the essential element in Tuscan cooking. Difficult though it would be, I can imagine a meal without wine but not without olive oil. That is why, although olives are the last crop in the Tuscan agricultural cycle, I begin the book with their harvest.

Olive oil poured over a generous slice of saltless bread and a glass of red wine symbolize the Tuscan table. I have written only of that most Tuscan of wines, Chianti and in particular, Chianti from the Classico region (a case in point of staying in my own backyard). Tuscany produces several other red and also white wines, Brunello de Montalcino, Vino Nobile di Montepulciano and Vernaccia di San Gimignano, to mention only the most reknowned. Two recent books treat Tuscan wines in detail, *The Wine Atlas of Italy*, written by Burton Anderson, my neighbour and fellow American, and *Chianti and the Wines of Tuscany* by Rosemary George, an English Master of Wine. That two of the most authoritative and comprehensive books on the subject have been written by foreigners is indicative of the status of Italian wines today.

A word about point of view. From the many windows of my apartment I look out upon archetypal Tuscan countryside. Sometimes I feel as if I am living inside the landscape of a Renaissance painting. From my study, where I tend to spend a lot of time staring out the window, I contemplate an olive grove, the leaves quicksilver in the winter light, and in the distance a medieval castle and hilltop hamlet. My sitting room has a view of vineyards running down gentle slopes towards a bend in the Arbia river that divides historical Chianti from the ancient territory of Siena. In summer the lush green of the vines contrasts with the burnt brick soil and with the myriad yellow sunflowers that look up from the fields below. From their room my guests can enjoy the first blossoms of spring in the orchard across the way and during harvest time watch the activity up at the winery. While I cook I see a corner of a Renaissance villa and the old garden wall out of which caper bushes trail their bluish green leaves. The old count, my landlord, who died while I was writing these pages, used to pick their buds and preserve them in salt. His wife used them to season her sauces.

I think the argument could be made that like the

Tuscan farm houses, topped with
characteristic dovecots.

Viewed from the author's window, a medieval tower still guards the historic boundary between the territories of Florence and Siena.

landscape, archetypal Italian cooking is Tuscan. Other regions have a more sophisticated cuisine, a greater variety of ingredients and dishes. Yet, Tuscan cooking is the purest, the most balanced, the essential. I think that is why any variations on the tradition provoke such a strong reaction. I have often heard the comment, when a cook has tried some minor innovation, that it might very well be tasty but it is not Tuscan. I cannot imagine the same remark being made in Bologna or Rome.

Tuscan cooking has its roots in the country. It is tied to the land and conditioned by the seasons. This is why it is often regarded as rustic, even frugal. It can be monotonous but when the new seasonal produce arrives in the market, you feel it a feast. The goodness of Tuscan dishes depends on the high quality of their ingredients, simply and sagely prepared, far more than on the skills of a chef. Following the seasons, I try to explain how the principal foods of Tuscany are produced and prepared for the table, describing along the way the people and places involved. The recipes are intended as another form of illustrating the subject matter. Some are typically Tuscan of the most orthodox type contributed by family cooks. Others are classic but have been intelligently and successfully 'reinterpreted', as they say in Italy nowadays, by professional chefs.

There is no essential difference between Tuscan home cooking and fine restaurant food. The latter is always judged in the light of the former. I have sat in on more than a couple of conversations where cooks and customers alike have discussed the best way to prepare a certain dish and their ultimate criterion is always how their mothers made it. Men, rather than women, seem to be the authority on this subject.

It is not easy to extract recipes from either Tuscan housewives or restaurant cooks. Not, as one might imagine, because they are jealous of their dishes. On the contrary, they are generous and enthusiastic in sharing their successes. It is simply that their recipes are part of an oral rather than a written tradition. Italian cooks prefer to work with their senses, sight, smell, touch and taste, rather than follow written instructions for weights and measurements, cooking times and procedures.

I am unabashedly an admirer of restaurateurs who have a sense of responsibility for the quality of the food they serve their clients. I stand in awe of their energy, dedication, generosity, the long hours at work and the constant care it takes to maintain high standards of ingredients, cooking and hospitality. One of the pleasures in writing this book has been the opportunity to pay homage to some of Tuscany's finest.

It is the Tuscans themselves who give particular savour to the pleasures of their table. They are, perhaps, the most reserved of their race but also the most gracious to the guest in their country. I am grateful for their hospitality and for the privilege of sharing their incomparable heritage.

Inevitably the foreign resident in Tuscany is a romantic and I personally believe in putting on rose-coloured glasses when travelling anywhere. Nevertheless, this does not prevent me from seeing that the reality is not always rosy. I forgot to mention that along those picturesque cypress crested hills I see from my window, phalanxes of ugly apartment blocks are visible on the horizon, approaching from the direction of Siena. One of my favourite restaurants is located in a beautiful hamlet where locals have lived and worked since medieval times and which now is being turned into a 'Holiday Village.' The waters surrounding the island of Elba are crystal clear but by all reports much of the sea along the Tuscan coast is ailing.

I can report with much satisfaction, however, the state of the art of cooking and the production of fine food products in Tuscany is very healthy indeed. It is easy to eat well here and (although increasingly difficult,) still possible to do so at a reasonable cost. Even when the price is high, you *almost* always get good value for the money. Finally, the most encouraging discovery I made while writing this book: to an extent that has amazed me, the present and the future of this tradition is in the competent young hands of an enthusiastic, respectful and hard-working generation.

Il Frantoio, the Olive Mill, where the author lives.

WINTER

It was a late November day when I arrived in Tuscany, just in time to help harvest the olives. In the hills of Chianti the landscape was luminous under a warm, golden light. The locals had stripped to the waist for work and I put on a Panama hat to protect my Celtic skin from the sun.

HARVESTING & PRESSING OLIVES FOR OIL

It was a late November day when I arrived in Tuscany, just in time to help harvest the olives. I had visited this area for years and now I had finally come to live. Only three days before I had been skidding down icy country roads on my way out of the dismally cold Welsh hills where I had felt snowed-in for what seemed like the better part of two years. In the hills of Chianti the landscape was luminous under a warm, golden light. The locals had stripped to the waist for work and I put on a Panama hat to protect my Celtic skin from the sun.

That was some fifteen years ago. Since then I have picked olives in chillier temperatures and have needed a wool cap to keep my head warm. I remember one year groping around in the snow with numb fingers in an attempt to help friends salvage what we could of their frost-bitten crop.

In upper Chianti where I live, most olive groves are planted on hillsides at altitudes ranging from 350 to 450 metres, unusually high for a Mediterranean fruit. The trick is to let the olives ripen on the tree for as long as possible but not so long that they might be nipped by the first frost.

Here the harvesting must be done by hand. In warmer, more southernly climes they simply lay the nets under the trees and let the olives ripen until the glossy black fruit is so heavy with juice it drops from the trees or can easily be shaken off. The species of olive tree that can survive at Chianti altitudes produces olives that never mature to that oily fatness but rather remain a lean redish ripe firmly attached to their branches. The pickers sling a basket over their shoulder that hangs by a cord at the waist, leaving both hands free for picking. They then climb up into the trees on rickety wooden ladders and with a little handheld rake comb the mahogany-coloured olives off their silver branches into the basket. The more seasoned workers use their bare, hardened hands.

During that first warm winter harvest of my arrival here, I remember Giovanni and Mario, the two farmhands on the estate where I was living, singing across the hill to Vilda, who was picking in the neighbouring grove. She would answer back. The curious rhythm of their alternating songs reminded me of a Gregorian chant. I could not remember the Prices and the Lewises of the Welsh hills ever singing while they sheared their sheep.

When their basket is full, the pickers pour the olives into large sacks that at the end of the day they carry up to a cool room in the barn. The olives are stored here until the full harvest is ready to be brought to the *frantoio*, the mill where they will be crushed and pressed for oil. Since freshly picked olives kept in piles for more than a few days begin to ferment, adversely affecting the odour and taste of their oil, conscientious, larger producers make several trips to the mill. With everyone moving fast to get their crop crushed, the *frantoio* schedules pressings twenty-four hours a day during the several weeks the picking season lasts.

Our local *frantoio* is just a few miles up the road from where I live, and I make a point of going there at least once during the season just to watch the activity. The place bustles and the air is pungent with the aroma of crushed olives. Farmers arrive in their pick-ups with bulging sacks of olives. Others depart with new oil in stainless-steel containers. Each one follows his harvest through every step of the milling process to make sure nobody's inferior olives get mixed in with his prime specimens and that, at the end, he gets

Harvesting olives by hand on the
estate of Cacchiano in Chianti,
producers of fine extra-virgin olive oil.

every last drop of the precious green-gold liquid. The temperature is kept several degrees warmer inside than out to keep the oil flowing, and one imagines that a fair amount of *grappa* has gone down to keep the momentum going. The tile-lined walls and floor, the machinery and the mill workers themselves, like Turkish wrestlers, glisten with oil.

After the olives are weighed in, they enter from the top floor by way of an outside conveyor belt and fall down a wooden shoot through a funnel, which catches excess leaves and twigs, and then into the mill itself. The base of the mill is a huge round granite slab. The olives, seeds and all, are crushed into a mash under two enormous vertical stones also of granite, each weighing about eight tons. In the old days, these stones were turned by a horse or ox. Today it is done by machinery.

In a process that reminds me of a pastry chef spreading icing between the layer of an enormous wedding cake, the mash is released through a tube onto large circular mats, originally of hemp but now made of nylon. These mats oozing with mash are stacked about eighty high with a metal disc inserted at every fifth mat for stability and are then put under a hydraulic press that exerts hundreds of tons of force on them. The oil drains down through the weave of the mats into a trough.

The next step in this ancient process is the only concession my local *frantoio* makes to modern technology. The oil is collected and placed in a centrifuge which spins out the natural water contained in the liquid. In former times the water was allowed to settle to the bottom over a period of weeks and the oil was skimmed off by hand. This process is called *sfioratura*, literally 'deflowering', and it is still

done, usually to the household reserve of the producer. Although superior results are claimed, I cannot taste a difference.

Oil from hand-picked olives cultivated at the high altitude of upper Chianti pressed in this traditional way is relatively rare and expensive even here. It is a labour-intensive, low-yield process. If the producer gets back eighteen kilos of oil from a hundred kilos of olives he considers it a good year. An old rule of thumb calculated that a kilo of this oil should cost the same as a kilo of the best beef, at a time when meat was a Sunday extravagance. At today's prices it works out to be less expensive and a little lasts longer than a steak. Since it is a monounsaturated fat – without any cholesterol – it is also healthier. A decisive indication of its value is the attitude of the pickers. They prefer to be paid not in cash but in kind.

I have come to appreciate this delicious golden-green oil as the best in the world. It is fresh and fruity both to the nose and on the palate, and has a distinctive and pleasingly peppery aftertaste that softens with time, characteristic of oil pressed from under-ripe olives. Around here it is simply referred to as *olio di frantoio*, oil from the mill, to distinguish it from the oils produced by the large industrial refineries. More technically it is often described as oil from the first, cold pressing of the olives. Refineries use chemical and heat processes to extract oil from *sansa*, the mash left over from the first cold pressing that they buy from the *frantoio*.

According to Italian law the highest qualification for olive oil is extra virgin, a classification that not only occasions rude remarks about Italian maidens but also does not always guarantee quality to the consumer. Extra virgin on the label ensures that the oil was produced by mechanical pressing, not extracted chemically, and has less than one per cent acidity. Acidity is what gives oil that disagreeable fatty taste which coats the mouth. However, an oil that has close to one per cent acidity will still taste quite fatty – the best 'extra-virgins' will have less than one half per cent acidity – and chemically refined oils can be de-acidified by adding alkaline solutions.

The only sure proof I know of the quality of an oil is *la prova del pane*, the bread test. In the *frantoio* of Brolio Castle, where I experienced the traditional process of making olive oil for the first time, there was a room in back with an open fireplace. The locals gathered here with some of their new oil fresh from the press. Each had also brought along a flask of his new wine, a pure, purple, potent juice much preferred to the sophisticated *Riservas* of the famous estates, a chunk of course, country bread and a head of garlic. Here I was introduced to the *prova del pane*, or the ritual of the *fettunta*, a simple ceremony that celebrates the fruit of the olive harvest.

Fettunta literally means 'oiled slice'. These men cut a piece of bread from their loaf, grilled it over the fire, rubbed it with a clove of garlic and doused the slice with new oil. Eating it was a feast that satisfied all the senses, the rich green-gold colour, the pungent aroma, the peppery taste and the oil that anointed your fingers. Since that day I have had *fettunta* adorned with tomatoes or *rucola* or mushrooms but none as memorable as that elemental slice eaten before the open fire of the *frantoio*. It was, as Lawrence Durrell described, 'a taste older than meat, older than wine. A taste as old as cold water'.

The local *frantoio* at Villa a Sesta does not have a backroom where this primeval rite takes place but as

luck would have it, practically across the street is La Bottega del 30. The proprietor, Franco Camelia, is the type who would not mind at all if you wanted to try your new oil in his restaurant, as long as you gave him a taste, too. His wife, Helène Stoquelet, makes a first class *fettunta*, along with a number of other dishes which feature *olio 'bono' del frantoio*, as Franco never fails to remind his guests.

Even before I first stepped inside La Bottega del 30 I knew I was going to like it. There was no sign announcing it to be a restaurant, and yet it was packed. Some seven years later there is still no sign, only the name embroidered on the linen curtains that hang in the window, and it is still always full.

Franco, a Sienese (and former goldsmith), and Helène, a Parisian who still finds time to teach French several hours a week in Siena ('Helps keep my perspective,' she says), decided ten years ago to move to the country. Several years later they opened a restaurant in the abandoned farmyard and building

Villa a Sesta, home to the area's olive mill and La Bottega del 30 (first building in centre foreground)

Franco Camelia, proprietor, and
Heléne Stoquelet, chef, of La
Bottega del 30

local ingredients prepared without any of the sauces but with all the subtlety of her native land. *Gli spaghetti del pastore* is a miracle of simplicity, dressed with grated garlic and aged *pecorino* cheese, *olio 'bono'* and freshly ground pepper. The main courses are the kind that take tender, loving care; stuffed rabbit and wild pigeon, braised beef and pork, meats roasted in the old courtyard oven flavoured with the scent of burning olive, juniper and oak. For dessert I usually head straight for Helène's *torta al cioccolato*, a transalpine secret best described as a baked mousse. By the end of the meal the table is decorated with an array of differently shaped and coloured glasses from Franco's impressive collection, the last additions containing a taste of dried fruits marinated in *grappa*.

A good place to end the evening is back in the little piazza in front of the *frantoio* at the tiny village store and café. On a clear winter night, across kilometres of hills planted in vineyards and olive groves, you can see the lights of Siena sparkling in the distance. Here two other young refugees from city life, Paolo and Enrico, serve a superior selection of digestive drinks. The locals drop in for a night cap, and I like to linger over a *grappino* before taking the road back home.

The Fundamental Fettunta, better known as Bruschetta

Fettunta and *bruschetta* are two words for the same dish. The difference is one of emphasis. The Tuscan term, *fettunta*, literally means an oiled slice (of bread), whereas the etymology of the Roman and now internationally adopted word, *bruschetta*, refers to burning, or better, charring the bread.

adjoining their house. Helène knew how to cook and Franco knew how to eat and they both enjoyed entertaining friends in the evening over a bottle or two of good wine.

There were only seven or eight tables then and there are only seven or eight tables now. Judging by the number of people they constantly turn away it is obvious this is one of those rare establishments that is not a business first of all but a way of life. Theirs was never an amateurish operation. They have applied their taste and talent with a diligence and dedication that was professional from the start. And the restaurant keeps getting better.

The inspiration for Helène's cooking is definitely Tuscan. Her dishes are based on simple, seasonal,

Originally *bruschetta* was probably a way to eat old bread. I think of *fettunta* as a way of *eating* fresh olive oil. Put in another way, one is a question of 'this bread could use a little olive oil to soften it up' (*bruschetta*); the other, 'this little pool of delicious olive oil needs some bread to wipe it up' (*fettunta*).

It seems silly to give detailed instructions for eating olive oil but a few general guidelines for preparing a fundamental *fettunta* might not be out of place.

The bread should be country-style, preferably a day or two old so it will not become soggy. It should be cut about 1 inch/2.5cm thick so the slice will support a generous dousing with oil.

Traditionally, and ideally, the bread should be grilled on both sides over the embers of a fire. Grilling (broiling) it on top of the stove is better than putting it in a toaster which really does not do the job. Rub the bread well with a clove of garlic while it is still hot so the garlic melts into the bread. If you are a devotee of 'the stinking rose,' you can rub it onto both sides of the bread. Because Tuscan bread is unsalted, Tuscans add a little salt at this point. Finally, pour on abundantly the best cold-pressed, extra virgin olive oil you can find.

At La Bottega del 30 Helène serves three *bruschetta* (half slices) on the same plate, this classic version and the two traditional variations that follow.

Bruschetta al Pomodoro

TOMATO *BRUSCHETTA*

The most basic tomato *bruschetta* is made simply by slicing a ripe tomato in half and rubbing one half *into* a piece of grilled garlicky bread and then adding salt and olive oil. In the following version you do not need to rub the bread with garlic since it has already added its flavour to the sauce. Place a bowl of the tomato sauce on the table and let your guests spoon the sauce over their bread.

Serves 6.
500g/1lb ripe tomatoes
2 cloves garlic, finely chopped
1 small handful fresh basil leaves, finely chopped
1 tbsp/15ml dried oregano
1 pinch chilli pepper
8fl oz/250ml (1 cup) extra virgin olive oil, or enough to cover the tomatoes
6 slices countrystyle bread
salt and pepper

Soak the tomatoes in boiling water for a couple of minutes, then cool in cold water and peel. Chop them into little pieces and place in a bowl with the garlic, basil, oregano, chilli pepper and olive oil. Marinate at room temperature for a couple of hours.

Right before serving, grill (broil) the bread. Place each slice on an individual plate and top with the tomato sauce.

Basic *bruschetta* with garlic and olive oil and two variations, with cauliflower and with tomato.

Creamed chick-pea soup with croutons.

Boil the cauliflower with the leaves in a pot of lightly salted water for 10-15 minutes. Drain well, reserving some of the liquid.

Right before serving, grill (broil) the bread and rub with the garlic. Place each slice on a plate and moisten with a little of the cauliflower cooking liquid.

Slice the cauliflower florets (flowerettes) into 6 thin pieces with some leaf attached on each, then place on the bread slices. Season each slice with a generous amount of olive oil, vinegar, salt and pepper.

Passato di Ceci con Gli Zoccoli
CREAMED CHICK-PEA SOUP WITH CROÛTONS

Zoccoli are horses hoofs as well as clogs. Here they refer to the deep-fried bread cubes. In Tuscany bread is sacred and it is seriously considered sinful to waste it. This was a way of using even the crumbs from the table.

Serves 6.
14oz/400g (2 cups) dried chickpeas
1 large carrot, peeled and roughly chopped
1 celery stick, chopped
1 large onion, peeled
3 ripe tomatoes, peeled and roughly chopped
1 garlic clove, very finely chopped
1 sprig fresh rosemary, very finely chopped
6 slices stale countrystyle bread, diced for croûtons
extra-virgin olive oil to taste
salt and pepper

Soak the chick peas in cool water over night. When ready to cook, drain them and rinse under cold running water. Put in a large pan with 5 pints/3 litres (3 quarts) water. Add the carrot, celery, onion and

Bruschetta al Cavolfiore
CAULIFLOWER *BRUSCHETTA*

For added flavour Helène recommends boiling the head of cauliflower with the inner leaves still attached. It should be cooked to the point where the florets (flowerettes) are still firm and can be thinly sliced from the head without crumbling. You should be able to detect the taste of the vinegar in this dish.

Serves 6.
1 cauliflower head with inner leaves attached
salt and pepper
6 slices countrystyle bread
6 cloves garlic
extra-virgin olive oil to taste
red wine vinegar to taste

tomatoes and bring to the boil for 10 minutes, then simmer for about 2 hours, skimming as necessary. When they are tender, drain, saving a little of the cooking liquid, and remove the vegetables.

Pass the chickpeas through a food mill, adding a little liquid as necessary, or purée in a blender or food processor. Add the garlic and rosemary to the chickpea purée and bring to the simmer, stirring continuously with a wooden spoon for about 5 minutes. Season with salt.

Deep-fry the cubes of bread in olive oil. Add about 1 tablespoon of croûtons to each bowl of soup just before serving. Drizzle with olive oil and add freshly ground black pepper.

White bean soup ladled over grilled bread.

Zuppa alla Frantoiana
WHITE BEAN SOUP WITH OLIVE OIL

Zuppa is thick soup ladled over bread. Locally this dish is also known as *zuppa alla Lombarda*, although what it has to do with the Lombards, nobody seems to know. If another vegetable, such as cauliflower, is added, it is called *zuppa bastarda*. The bread must be hard so it will not absorb all the liquid and become soggy.

Serves 6.
7oz/200g (1 cup) dried cannellini beans
7 cloves garlic
1 carrot, peeled and roughly chopped
1 onion, peeled
1 celery stick, roughly chopped
2 fresh sage leaves
6 thin slices very stale countrystyle bread
extra-virgin olive oil to taste
red wine vinegar to taste
salt and pepper

It is customary in Tuscany not to soak the beans but to cook them in abundant water. Put the beans, 1 clove of garlic, the carrot, onion and sage in a large pan of water. Bring to the boil for 10 minutes, then simmer for about 2 hours, skimming as necessary, until tender. Season.

Right before serving, grill (broil) the bread and rub each slice with 1 clove garlic. Arrange the bread in 2 or 3 pieces in 6 individual deep plates or shallow bowls and pour over a ladlefull of cooking liquid. Top the bread with beans, then drizzle each portion with extra-virgin olive oil, not more than 2 drops of vinegar and freshly ground black pepper.

SWEETS FROM SIENA

With any luck you can still make it to the second week of December in Tuscany without being assaulted by commercial Christmas cheer. Traditionally, the eighth of December, the feast of the Immaculate Conception of the Blessed Virgin Mary, one of the few religious holy days that has remained on the calendar of legal holidays as well, marks the beginning of the season. Street and window decorations go up in the large cities but most small towns and villages mercifully maintain a wintry 'silent night, holy night' atmosphere until just a few days before the feast.

Siena, my hometown, is particularly splendid at Christmas time. Not that its aspect changes much – Siena does not need to be dressed up for the occasion – but what is always there assumes a spirit eminently suited to the season. There is no civic Christmas tree in sight but the agile and elegant illuminated tower of the town hall rises over 328 feet/100 metres into the inky blue sky, silent and solitary, above a deserted Piazza del Campo, certainly one of the most beautiful open spaces in the world. And few cities in Europe are crowned with an ornament more striking than the cathedral of Santa Maria, striped with broad Byzantine bands of white and dark-green marble. Siena has no need to put up Christmas cribs. Many of Western civilization's most sublime portrayals of the Madonna and Child, and other scenes associated with the mysteries of Christmas, were painted by the great masters of the Sienese school of late medieval and Renaissance art.

Perhaps the most stunning and one of the most precious masterpieces of the Middle Ages is the monumental *Maestà* of Duccio di Buoninsegna, originally the high alterpiece of the cathedral and now in its own room in the cathedral museum. Against a gold background, Mary, completely wrapped in a dark blue mantle and holding her child, is seated on a marble throne draped with an embroidered red-gold cloth. They are surrounded by adoring angels and saints but her gentle and luminous gaze is focused inwards.

Along *Via di Città*, the city's central street, a festive glow emanates from the coloured cut-glass panels in the mullioned windows of its magnificent gothic palaces. A window-shopping stroll will give you a foretaste of the feasting to come. At No. 93, Pizzicheria De Miccoli, with a boar's head sporting specs greeting you at the entrance, garlands of sausages are strung and hung with great thighs of *prosciutto* and *salame*. The counter is piled with rounds of *pecorino* cheese and, in the centre, an enormous basket is filled with fragrant dried *porcini* mushrooms. A little further along, Drogheria Manganelli, illuminated within by nineteenth-century crystal beaded chandeliers, displays, along with 'teas and other drugs', including alcohol, every imaginable gayly wrapped bon-bon for Christmas stockings (which Italian children do not hang by the chimney until January 5th, the eve of the feast of the Epiphany). Towards the end of the street is the elegant delicatessen Morbidi, where well-coiffed women in fur coats buy perfectly prepared dishes to take home for their pre-Christmas parties.

Should you walk in the other direction from the cathedral, down *Via dei Fusari*, you will see a Sienese Christmas speciality in preparation. Pasticceria Bini has three large windows fronting the street that allow you to watch while a team of pastry chefs mix, pour and bake the batter for *panforte*.

The splendid shapes of Siena's Duomo
rise above buildings of burnt sienna.

Dusk silhouettes Siena's skyline,
unchanged for almost a
thousand years.

Panforte is a cake made with fruit and spices, although to call it a 'fruitcake' would be, to turn a phrase of Marcella Hazan's regarding *polenta* and porridge, 'a most indelicate use of the language'. According to a relatively recent tradition from the seventeenth century, *panforte* should be composed of seventeen ingredients, just as the city of Siena is composed of seventeen *contrade* or wards: honey, sugar, crystalized melon, citron, orange and lemon rinds (peels), walnuts, hazelnuts, almonds, coriander, cinnamon, cloves, nutmeg, mace, pepper, flour, water and heat. Its name, which means 'pungent bread,' describes its spicy aroma and taste. In consistency it is dense and chewy but not hard.

The origin of *panforte* is enveloped in early medieval mist but in its present form it can be documented back to the thirteenth century when Siena was at the height of her glory. Before that time *panforte* was the generic name for bread derived from earlier honey breads, *panes melatos*, mixtures of honey, flour and water, to which fruit and nuts had been added. When the crusaders brought back spices from the Middle East, these rare and exotic commodities were eventually added to *panforte*, which then became known as *panpepato*, pepper bread, called after one of its most valued ingredients.

Who first came up with the idea of peppering their bread is a matter of conjecture. In all probability it was some *speziale*, the medieval predecessor of the pharmacist. In those days spices were prized primarily for their medicinal properties. The profession of *speziale* was frequently exercised by nuns and monks who occupied themselves with the health of the body as well as the soul. A document dated 1205, from a monastery of cloistered Camaldolese nuns located on the outskirts of Siena, mentions the excellent *panpepato* prepared by the sisters. Up until the nineteenth century *panforte* was made and sold not in bakeries but in the pharmacies of Siena. The now-famous brands of *panforte*, *Parenti*, *Sapori* and *Pepi*, were originally family names of pharmacists. You can still see *Panforte* painted in gold letters on one of the eighteenth-century poly-chrome glass cabinets in the lovely old pharmacy of the *Piazza del Campo*. It was not until 1829, that the pharmacist Giovanni Parenti founded the first *panforte* factory in Siena.

Over the centuries it seems the Sienese lost their taste for the piquant, peppery bread that was so pleasing to their medieval and Renaissance forebears. The dosage of spices was gradually lessened and then, chocolate, as well as marzipan, were added to the ancient *panforte* formula. In 1879, when Margherita di Savoia and her husband, Umberto, king and queen of Italy, visited Siena for the Palio, Enrico Righi, proprietor of the *Panforte Parenti* factory, created a *panforte bianco* for the occasion, less spicy and lighter in colour, texture and taste than the traditional dark *panforte nero*, covered it with a veil of icing (confectioners') sugar, and called it *panforte Margherita*. (Ten years later, in Naples, the same royal personage would also have a pizza named after her.)

Right: A syrup of candied fruit, honey and sugar is blended into a mixture of flour, nuts and spices to make the dough for *panforte*.

From that time on, *panforte Margherita* became synonymous for this Sienese sweet.

Then, in 1965, Danilo Nannini, now president of the company founded by his father, Guido Nannini, in 1937, that produces not only Siena's best pastry and ice cream but also the city's finest *panforte*, had the happy idea of re-introducing the ancient *panpepato*. Going against the popular trend, he judged that the more aromatic and savoury flavours of the traditional recipe would entice contemporary tastes. He consulted local food historians, researched archives for recipes and spoke with elderly, retired bakers who could recall older versions of *panforte nero* and finally came up with the formula for Nannini *panpepato*.

His intuition proved correct. When I took an informal poll among my Sienese friends, they unanimously rated Nannini *panpepato* their favourite. I suspect this is due not only to the quality of the product but also because *Nannini* is a household name in Siena. Their three cafès and pastry shops are lively city institutions, and two of the younger generation are international celebrities. Alessandro Nannini is a successful Formula One race car driver and Gianna Nannini is a European rock star.

Although thirty employees, whose number swells to eighty during the pre-Christmas rush, now make over 160 tons annually, the several types of *panforte* Nannini remain very much a hand-made product. The storerooms look and smell like a caravansari, stacked with boxes and brimming sacks of candied fruit, nuts and spices, all of the highest quality. The almonds from Puglia are considered the best in the world for cooking because of their sweet flavour and high degree of essential oil. The citron comes from an area along the coast of Calabria, where this fruit is prized for its smooth and compact aromatic rind (peel). The melon is grown under the hot sun of Campania and the orange and lemon rinds (peel) are from the fruit of the finest groves in Sicily.

The workshop is dominated by three huge copper cauldrons. Here the mix of candied fruit, honey, sugar and water is heated to about 279°F/115°C. This syrup is then transfered to another container where the flour, nuts and spices are added and mixed into a dough. The exact dosage of spices that goes into *panpepato* is kept a closely guarded secret of the Nannini family. Sergio Broggi, the young director of production, tells me that when he decides it is time to bake a fresh batch, he telephones Danilo Nannini in the city and either he or his wife, Giovanna, grind and mix the required amount of spices and send it down to the factory.

When the dough has been kneaded to the right consistency it is rolled in flour and moulded by hand into ring shaped forms of five different sizes, ranging from a small 3½oz/100g disc to a large round weighing 2lb/1kg. These are then placed on a conveyor belt that carries them into a large industrial oven where they are baked for about twenty-five minutes. After cooling overnight, they are sealed in a special aluminium foil which keeps them fresh for at least eight months. *Panpepato* is then hand-wrapped in a heavy, coarsely grained old-yellow paper and tied with cord that is fixed to the package with a red wax seal embossed with an 'N' in medieval script. For their cafè-pastry shops, Nannini also bakes *panforte* in enormous 10 pound/5 kilo rounds. You can buy a large slice by weight or a sliver to enjoy with a cup of cappucino or a glass of Vin Santo at the bar.

Christmas is a time to tell stories about mysterious

'Sugar and spice and all things nice,'
including pepper, is what Nannini
Panpepato is made of.

and wonderful events. A Sienese friend recounted for me a tale her grandmother used to tell her every Christmas eve, which she in turn told her children and they will certainly tell theirs. It goes like this:

'Once upon a time, on a snowy winter night, a little shepherd boy returning home saw a stable illuminated by a brilliant star. Inside he found a baby lying in the manger and three splendidly dressed kings from the Orient offering him precious gems and exotic spices.

'The little shepherd also wanted to give something to this new-born baby who seemed even poorer than himself but all he had in his pocket were a few crumbs left over from his frugal lunch, a morsel of honey bread and some pieces of fruit and nuts. Everything had gotten squishy and squashed together as bits and pieces tend to do in little boys' pockets.

'The little shepherd did his best to pat it all together into a presentable shape and then very shyly offered his gift to the baby's mother, who gave him such a warm smile of gratitude he forgot his embarrassment. When she took his gift into her hands it turned a golden brown, the fruit gleamed like precious stones and produced an aroma even more marvellous than the spices of the Magi. She broke off a piece of this miraculous cake for him to eat and it was the most delicious sweet he ever tasted.'

The boys down at my local bar have their own way of keeping alive the Christmas *panforte* tradition. During the holiday season they play a game in which the contestants toss, frisbee style, a disc of *panforte* some 25 feet/7.5 metres across the room in an attempt to land it on a table at the other side. Whoever succeeds in placing it closest to the far edge of the tabletop wins. The prize? A *panforte*, of course!

At Nannini the dough for *panforte* is kneaded by hand, rolled in flour and moulded into shape before baking.

Panpepato

PEPPER CAKE

Sergio Broggi, director of production at *Nannini Panforte*, composed this recipe for *panpepato*, adapting it to the home kitchen.

Serves 6.
6oz/180g (scant 1 cup) granulated sugar
2oz/60g (2½tbsp) acacia honey
¾oz/20g caramelized sugar
7oz/200g crystallized (candied) orange peel
3½oz/100g crystallized (candied) citron
7oz/200g (heaped 1 cup) unblanched almonds
2tbsp unsweetened cocoa
pinch freshly ground black pepper
pinch chilli powder
pinch grated nutmeg
pinch ground cinnamon
5oz/150g (1¼ cups) plain (all-purpose) flour

Combine the sugar, honey, and caramelized sugar and 5fl oz/150ml (⅔ cup) water in a saucepan. Bring to the boil, stirring slowly. Boil the syrup until the surface is covered with fairly large bubbles (about 250°F/121°C).

Remove from the heat and add the crystallized (candied) fruit and almonds along with the cocoa and spices, stirring well. Gradually stir in the flour and mix until the batter is well blended but still sticky.

Transfer the mixture to a 9inch (23cm) springform pan. Press down and smooth the mixture with the palm of your hand, then dredge lightly with flour and bake in a pre-heated 400°F/200°C/Gas mark 6 oven for about 20 minutes.

Remove the cake from the oven and leave it to cool on a wire rack at room temperature for about 4 hours. Brush the flour off the top and sprinkle lightly with extra cocoa mixed with a pinch of black pepper.

Ricciarelli alla Mandorla

— ALMOND BISCUITS (COOKIES) —

This is another traditional sweet of Siena whose origins go back to the Middle Ages. Formerly *ricciarelli* were made in convents, and a friend told me they are still sometimes naughtily called 'nuns' thighs'. This recipe was contributed by Sergio Broggi of Nannini.

Makes about 36.
7oz/200g (heaped 1 cup) blanched sweet almonds
2tbsp blanched bitter almonds
7oz/200g (1 cup) granulated sugar
2oz/60g (2½tbsp) acacia honey
2 egg whites
drop vanilla essence (extract)
2 tsp/10ml baking powder
1tbsp/15ml grated orange rind (peel)
2oz/60g (½ cup) vanilla-flavoured or plain icing (confectioners') sugar

Soak both types of almonds in lukewarm water for about 30 minutes. Drain the almonds and spread them out on a kitchen towel to dry.

Combine the almonds, sugar, egg whites and honey in a blender or food processor. Process until the almonds are pulverised and the mixture is well blended. Transfer the mixture to a bowl and leave it to rest for at least 12 hours.

Stir in the vanilla, baking powder and orange rind (peel), blending the ingredients.

Roll out the pastry on a board lightly sprinkled with icing (confectioners') sugar and divide it into pieces weighing about 1oz/30g each. Shape the pieces into lozenges about 2inches/5cm long and 1½ inches/4cm wide at the broadest point. Arrange the lozenges on a baking tray (cooked sheet) covered with grease-proof (waxed) or rice paper. Sprinkle the biscuits (cookies) with a thin layer of icing sugar and bake in a pre-heated 350°F/180°C/Gas mark 4 oven for about 18 minutes.

PROCESSING THE FAMILY PORKER & HUNTING FOR WILD BOAR

Throughout Tuscany, chiselled in stone and carved in marble on medieval churches, painted in the frescoes of Renaissance villas and engraved on the pages of antiquarian books, you come across depictions of men and women engaged in various activities linked with the annual agricultural cycle: sowing seed, harvesting wheat, picking grapes, even youth courting — the work force for future generations must be ensured. There is usually one panel for each month of the year. Come December, the farmer is often portrayed with his feet before the fire enjoying a winter's rest.

The most dramatic scene is January's. It shows the slaughter of the family pig. This is a ritual whose origins go back to the rite of Roman sacrifice. The fattened pig, symbol of plentitude, was offered in thanksgiving by the priests and its flesh cut-up and distributed to the populace.

Down through the centuries in north central Italy, especially Tuscany, where pork is the most esteemed of meats, every farmer singled out a piglet to fatten for his family. It would normally be a female, whose flesh is considered sweeter and more tender, and often the runt of the litter, which would have brought less money at market. It would be allowed to graze freely on spring grass and in autumn would be fed on acorns, pumpkins and chestnuts.

Then, during the rigidly cold days of deep winter, when the temperature provided the refrigeration necessary for the occasion, down from the Apennines came the *norcino*, a butcher who specialized in the making of pork products, to kill, bleed and process the parts of the pig into *prosciutto*, salami and sausage.

The annual arrival of the *norcino* inaugurated a family festivity that lasted three or four days and livened-up the dreary period between the Christmas holidays and *Carnevale*. On the morning of the first day the pig was bled and left to hang for a couple of days. Then the *norcino* returned to process the meat and on the last day, usually a Sunday, the family feasted. In my part of Tuscany this was called the *smaialata*, a word that nicely expresses the somewhat naughty merry making associated with piggish behaviour. When it was all over, the family larder was replenished for another year with nourishing and tasty foods.

Every winter my village butcher, Vincenzo Chini, doubles as a *norcino*, a fast disappearing trade he learned from his father. (The Chini family have been in the local butchering business for the past 300-years.) He is hired by the few remaining families in the area who still carry on the ancient tradition of the domestic slaughter of the pig. In cookery books you are often advised to 'make friends with your local butcher'. With affable, gregarious Chini this was easy to do. He was the first friend I made in the village and over the years he has brought me along on several of the festive occasions.

When Vincenzo arrives to slaughter the pig, the able-bodied men of the family have already gathered in the farmyard. The women are in the kitchen boiling water and making other preparations, while the children usually watch with me from a safe distance. In the past when the *norcino* plunged his long, double-edged knife into the arteries of the heart, this must have been a terrifying moment, both for the animal and the participants. Today the pig is tied by the snout, digs its hoves into the ground and a metal bolt is fired into its brain.

The porker falls to the ground and Vincenzo

Tuscan *prosciutto* is hung in a well-
ventilated room to age at least
eight months.

expertly bleeds it. The men collect the thick, rich blood in a huge terracotta bowl that the women bring up to the kitchen to refrigerate. It will be used later to make *buristo*, blood sausage. In some homes, where they just cannot wait to taste the first fruit of sacrifice, the women prepare a quick, mid-morning snack called *sanguinaccio*. This is a blood pudding cooked with breadcrumbs or sometimes sweet biscuit (cookie) crumbs and a pinch of Tuscan spices. I was lucky to have had a fairly easy initiation to this rite. The first time I participated the women of the house added beaten eggs to the blood and made a very palatable *frittata nera*, black omelette.

After the pig has been thoroughly bled, it is placed on a flat surface, sometimes a short wooden ladder that rests on a couple of improvized props. The women bring out pans of hot water and while one of the men pours water over the carcass, Vincenzo turns barber and shaves off the hair with a blunted edge of a knife.

When its skin is smooth and pink and the hooves have been removed, the pig is hoisted by means of a pulley system attached to a strong branch of a tree and hangs suspended a couple of feet off the ground. With a very sharp, short bladed knife, Vincenzo then slits open the belly, beginning from the groin and working down towards the head and then completely disembowels the animal. The women wash the intestines and later Vincenzo will adroitly turn this complex system of tubes inside out to use as casing for the sausage. He continues to cut the pig into two vertical halfs with the help of a cleaver to break the bones down the spine and stops short of the head. At this point the two parts of the pig are held together only by the tissue at the base of the skull.

For the benefit of the children, whom it amuses, and me, whom it startled the first time, Vincenzo concludes this part of the festivities with a little comic relief. He blows-up the bladder like a balloon. When it dries it becomes like plastic and will be used as a pouch to store pieces of lard.

By now everyone has worked-up an appetite and is ready for another snack, this time *tegamata*. The sweetbreads are sautéed in olive oil, seasoned with fennel and sampled right out of the pan (*tegame* in Italian), while purplish new wine is poured from the flask.

On the second day the household rises early. A good six hours of work and several of play lie ahead. In former times the job of processing the pork and the feasting on it were divided into two days. Now, when many members of a farming family have other employment as well, these activities are combined into one *festa*.

Vincenzo arrives about 7.30 am, carrying an impressive array of knives and his sausage maker. Next to his work what he most enjoys in life is a good party. Stocky and black bearded with a mischievous grin, Vincenzo also has a flair for the theatrical and has, in fact, stared in many a village comedy. Playing the part of *norcino* is certainly his finest role. He is an absolute wiz at his work and his ready wit for ribald repartee has plenty of scope and an appreciative audience, especially when it comes time to fill the salami and sausages.

The pig has already been laid out on a large marble top table in the cellar. It weighs about 200 pounds/100 kilos, and by the end of the day, in one way or another, Vincenzo will have disposed of it all, from ears to tail. With the sure, swift movements of a skilled surgeon he begins by dividing this 'meal on legs' into three sections: the hind, the centre and the fore.

He starts with the largest and most excellent cut, the two hind thighs, from which he will make *prosciutto*. With a razor-sharp knife he carves them into their characteristic shape. The trimmings are set aside and will be used for salami and sausage. In a huge mortar he pounds several heads of garlic with a pestle and rubs the creamy paste over the hefty thighs. Then he covers them with salt to cure for about two weeks (Tuscans prefer their *prosciutto* saltier than the sweeter ham from Parma), until his expert eye judges they are ready to be washed, rubbed with pepper and hung in a well-ventilated room to age for at least eight months.

From autumn through spring Vincenzo processes an average of four to five pigs a week and the fame of his *prosciutto* and other pork products is widespread. In his shop you can buy it by the slice or take home a whole one.

The front shoulder, called *spalla*, is shaped and cured in much the same way. Because a porker develops more muscle in this part of his body, the meat is less tender and *spalla* is less expensive than *prosciutto*.

Between the head and the shoulder lies an esteemed little cut weighing only about 6 pounds/3 kilos called *capocollo* in Tuscany and *coppa* further north. It, too, is cured in salt but just for a few days and seasoned with pepper. A couple of slices are always part of the traditional Tuscan *antipasto* platter of sliced cured pork meats. The meat is darker and has more fat and the flavour is more intense than *prosciutto*.

Next Vincenzo goes to work on the central section of the pig. He gives the loin to the women who will prepare *arista* for lunch. They roast it with olive oil, garlic and fennel or sometimes rosemary. A fifteenth-century Patriarch Bishop of Constantinople who was in Florence for an Ecumenical Council is said to have given this most delicious Tuscan roast its name. The story goes that when it was served to His Eminence he proclaimed it to be '*aristos*', Greek for the best.

Around about this time the ribs are thrown on the fire for a late morning snack, called *rosticciana* in Tuscany, and new wine from the flask begins to flow. Vincenzo carves away the belly leaving the skin intact to make *pancetta*. He cuts the layers of white fat and pink meat into thick bacon-like strips that will be hung in the larder and used during the year to flavour innumerable dishes. In his shop Vincenzo sells *pancetta arrotolata*, peeled of its skin, rolled up and flavoured with rosemary and juniper. In this form it is cooked like a roast. *Guanciale*, cured pig's jowl, is used to season dishes in the same way as *pancetta*.

Before lunch the men boil a huge cauldron of water over a fire in the courtyard. Into this pot go head, ears, tongue, tail, trotters and other bits and pieces. After

Vincenzo Chini carves a porker's hefty hind thigh into the characteristic shape of *prosciutto*.

they have simmered for about three hours, Vincenzo will make *soppressata*, a speciality of Siena, similar to brawn. The cooked meat is chopped into bits, seasoned with spices and orange rind (peel) and tightly pressed into a linen cloth, then tied and hung to cool. The lard that drips off is collected and much prized as a spread to put on warm grilled (broiled) bread. When it is unwrapped and cut, *soppressata* looks like a large marbled salami. It is eaten fresh, usually as an *antipasto*.

The classic appetizer for this special Sunday lunch are *ciccioli*, little cubes of lard fried in olive oil and wrung out in a cloth so that only the crunchy fibres remain. Vincenzo calls them Italian popcorn.

With after dinner coffee a couple glasses, at least, of *grappa* are downed to fortify the group before they return to the chilly cellar for the afternoon's labour. From the morning session Vincenzo has amassed about 50 pounds/25 kilos of cuttings that he now puts through his meat grinder. From these he will turn out about 30 pounds/15 kilos of *salame toscano*, 10 pounds/ 5 kilos of sausage and 10 pounds/5 kilos of *finocchiona*, a large, course-grained salami flavoured with wild fennel seeds. His salami are composed of approximately seventy-five per cent carefully selected lean bits of pork and the rest fat. They are seasoned with salt, ground and whole peppercorns, garlic and a glass of Chianti for good measure. The sausage mixture is half lean and half fat.

The specified proportions of ground pork are heaped into a huge pile on the table and everyone rolls up their sleeves and begins to pound and knead it down, repeating the operation until the meat begins to stick to their hands. Vincenzo says it will not have reached the desired consistency until the effort brings out a sweat. Then it is ready to be stuffed into its casing, pig's intestine for the sausages and larger veal intestine for salami. Using a cylindrical machine with a plastic tube at one end to which he attaches the intestine, he grinds the meat into the skin, ties the end with cord and pricks the salami all over with a little brush of nails to release any humidity during the period it has to dry, at least six months. Vincenzo's sausage is of such high and delicious quality that it can be eaten raw, cut open and spread on bread.

The last product to be processed from this generous pig was the first gift it gave. The terracotta bowl of blood is brought out and Vincenzo proceeds to make about 8 pounds/4 kilos of *buristo*, blood sausage. These are flavoured with salt, pepper, garlic and pieces of pork skin. Talented performer and artisan that he is, Vincenzo concludes with a spectacular grand finale. He makes the last blood sausage using the large intestine of the pig as casing. It comes out at least 3.2 feet/1 metre long and about 2½ inches/6cm wide, amid many a jest about its gigantic proportions. This sausage is called the *Pasqualino*. It is boiled for about 30 minutes and then stored in the cellar under ashes all winter and will be eaten by the family after Easter Sunday Mass.

Affettato Toscano
SLICED TUSCAN PORK MEATS

A plate of sliced pork meats is a traditional Tuscan *antipasto* in restaurants and for family mid-day meals on special occasions. More often they are eaten in a *panino*, a roll, for a mid-morning *merenda*, or snack. Rather than a recipe, this might serve as a shopping

Last rays of the winter sun warm a
dormant vineyard and ancient farm
buildings incongruously crowned with
neo-gothic battlements.

list glossary when buying a picnic lunch at a Tuscan butcher shop. Terminology and to some extent content vary according to area. All you need to add to your basket will be a loaf of Tuscan bread, some firm tomatoes and a bottle of Chianti.

Prosciutto toscano: taken from the hind thigh of the pig; in Tuscany cured with more salt than the more familiar Parma ham.

Salame toscano: salami with large 'eyes' of fat, usually flavoured with pepper and garlic.

Finocchiona: a course grained salami seasoned with wild fennel seeds.

Soppressata: a large marbled salami similar to brawn, made from the boiled head, ears, tongue, tail and trotters with spices and orange rind (peel).

Capocollo: a cut taken from the section between the head and the shoulder of the pig in Chianti, richer in flavour than *prosciutto*.

Spalla: cured shoulder cut; less tender (and less expensive) than *prosciutto*, it also has more bite.

Salsiccie fresche: these will not be part of an *antipasto* plate but high quality fresh Tuscan sausages are good for a picnic cut open and their contents spread on bread.

Salsiccie Toscane
TUSCAN SAUSAGES

This is Vincenzo Chini's recipe for home-made sausages. If sausage casing is not available, the mixture may be formed into patties and pan fried for about 6 minutes on each side. These sausages are often served with white beans (see page 126).

Makes 12.
1lb 3½oz/600g lean pork
7oz/200g unsmoked lean bacon
3½oz/100g unsmoked fatty bacon
1tbsp/15ml salt
1tsp/5ml freshly ground black pepper
2tsp/10ml mixed grated nutmeg, ground cloves, chilli pepper and ground cinnamon
3 cloves garlic, very finely chopped

Put the meat through a meat mincer (grinder) with a 2in/5cm blade or ask your butcher to mince (grind) it for you or use a food processor. Combine all the ingredients and mix together well. Turn the mixture into a work surface and knead, as you would bread, for 5 minutes.

Stuff a medium size sausage casing with the mixture. Twist into 12 sausages, tie the ends and hang from a hook in a cool place until required.

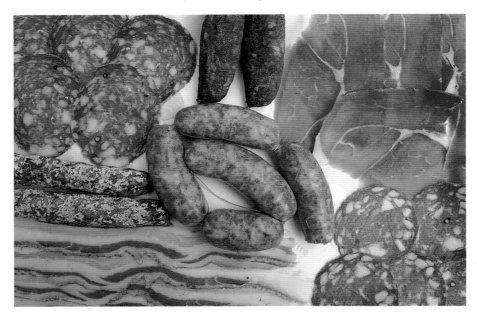

Sliced Tuscan pork meats and sausages. Clockwise from the top, wild boar sausage, *prosciutto*, salami, *pancetta*, blood sausage, *finocchiona*, and in the centre, links of fresh sausage.

Skewers of pork seasoned with fresh sage. The piece at the centre is pig's liver wrapped in caul net.

Spiedini di Maiale
TUSCAN SKEWERED PORK

When Grazia Chini, Vincenzo's wife, prepares these skewers for their shop, she wraps the pig's liver in caul net. She also assembles some without the liver and adds a couple pieces of chicken thigh or breast. If fresh sage is unavailable, crumble dry sage over the skewers before cooking.

Makes 6.
7oz/200g pork fillet (tenderloin)
7oz/200g pork liver
7oz/200g sweet Italian sausage
7oz/200g unsmoked bacon
2 yellow bell peppers, cored and seeded
(2fl oz/60ml (¼ cup) extra-virgin olive oil
18 fresh sage leaves
salt and pepper

Cut the various meats into pieces about 1½in (4cm) long and ½in (1cm) thick. Cut the peppers into pieces 1½in (4cm) long and more or less the same width as the meat. Brush the cut meat with olive oil, beaten with a pinch of salt.

When putting the meat on the skewers make sure that the pork liver is always between slices of bacon and sausage, as this prevents it from drying out during cooking. Place 3 pepper slices and 3 sage leaves on each skewer.

Grill over charcoal or hang the skewers over a roasting pan in a 350°F/180°C/Gas Mark 4 oven for about 30 minutes, then pour the cooking juices over the skewers before serving.

Part of a hunter's satisfaction is handling a finely crafted rifle.

it off anyway — as they do a number of other days during the three-month season. The shoot for smaller game — hare, pheasant, quail, partridge and even such tiny song birds as thrushes — starts in early autumn but the hunter's adrenalin does not really begin to flow until the chase for wild boar begins, the only 'big game' still plentiful in the Tuscan country-side.

Recently the hunters themselves have come under fire. There is a growing national movement to ban hunting altogether. Yet, the population of wild boar constitutes a major menace to crops in many areas. They are prolific and have an unerring nose for the ripest grapes. On a late summer's night it is not unusual to catch a pack of wild boar in your head-lights as they cross a country road on their way from one vineyard meal to another. In Chianti local authorities often give permission for an out-of-season shoot, much to the satisfaction of both hunters and growers. Then, of course, there is a convincing culinary argument in favour of the hunt. *Cinghiale in agrodolce*, wild boar stewed in a sweet and sour sauce of red wine vinegar and dark chocolate seasoned with bay, juniper berries and pine nuts, has been a classic of the Tuscan table at least since the Renais-sance. It is a delicacy that could sooth the conscience of all but the most unyielding conservationist.

In many parts of Tuscany the forest and brush that covered much of the land and provided ideal habitat for game has disappeared. There remains, however, a strip of largely wild and desolate terrain called the *Maremma* in the region's southernmost province of Grosseto, where the chase still flourishes. The diversity of this area, often referred to as 'the other Tuscany' is immediately apparent as you drive for

Another Tuscan ritual even more primitive than the slaughter of the domestic pig involves as principal the ancient ancestor of the family porker. Every year it seems I hardly get to bed after our Halloween party (a little imported culture from my native land), when I am awakened by a volley of shots echoing down the valley. It takes me a while to remember that November 1, the Feast of All Saints and a public holiday in Italy, is also the opening of the season for wild boar. Appropriately, November 2, is dedicated to the commeration of the dead.

After soccer, hunting is the favourite sport in Tuscany (mushrooming would be third), and if the first of November were not already a holiday, the majority of able-bodied men in the region would take

The *Maremma*, a land of plains and
low rolling hills, where wild boar and
other game flourish.

miles through marshy plains and low rolling hills without seeing an olive grove or vineyard. Places here remind me of the lonely prairies of the American West. The *Maremma* even has indigenous cowboys called *butteri*, who still roam the range wearing distinctive *borsalino*-style hats and carrying cowpokes used to herd the local breed of white, big-horned cattle.

The *Maremma* was originally territory of the Etruscans, the people who occupied central Italy before the Romans booted them out. The efficient system of canals the Etruscans had built to drain the flat plains were subsequently neglected and by medieval times the *Maremma* had become a breeding ground for malarial mosquitoes. In the nineteenth century the Austrian Grand Dukes of Tuscany began to reclaim the land but it was not until the American army introduced DDT to the area that the anopheles mosquito was exterminated.

Today the *Maremma* is once again a peaceful and prosperous land. It is bordered to the west by 82 miles/130 kilometres of largely unspoilt coastline that encompasses a nature park reserve for migratory birds, Monti dell'Uccellina. Many of the birds like it so much they stay the whole year — grey, white and red herons and ducks of every description. Once I thought I saw a flock of pink flamingoes but it might have been the effect of too much sun. About 12½ miles/20 kilometres inland on the north-east border is Monte Amiata, a sleeping volcano whose peak, often capped with snow, is the highest elevation in Tuscany south of Florence.

In between the mountains and the sandy beaches lined with sparse forests of parasol pines, the foothills are sprinkled with medieval hilltop towns, many with Etruscan and Roman ruins, built atop cliffs of volcanic rock. Pitigliano, Sorano and Massa Marittima are the most spectacular. The valley terrain is covered with *macchia*, Mediterranean scrub, rosemary, heather, juniper and thickets of arbutus and broom. This is the domain of fox, weasel, badger, porcupine, hedgehog, deer and, of course, the wild boar.

Years ago I agreed to accompany one of my nephews visiting from America on a boar hunt, just in case he was caught in a cross fire and needed the services of a translator. Wild boar move in packs and so do the hunters and their dogs. By law the human group is set at a minimum of thirty and a maximum of eighty. They are accompanied by at least fifteen to twenty yelping pooches, mostly a cross between bloodhound and beagle, friendly little fellows who are as excited as their masters at the prospects of a day out of confinement. One gets the definite impression that for the hunters the point of this exercise, apart from the trophy, is a day with the Boys.

In keeping with the best of Italian country custom, the morning begins with a *merenda*, a hearty brunch of bread, *prosciutto*, salami and grilled sausages washed down with enough new wine to fortify the system until a late lunch at sunset. Every team has its appointed hunting ground. A few scouts are sent ahead to stalk the territory for hoof tracks and telltale signs of rummaging in the earth in order to determine which zone to stake out and scour.

Then the team encircles that area, forming a corridor along the valley through which the boar will be forced to their destiny. At one end about five hunters with dogs begin to stalk the prey. The hoots and cries of the hunters on the side-lines attempting to rout the boar from under cover, combined with the frenetic barking of the hounds, can be heard for miles warning innocent civilians to keep a safe distance.

Notwithstanding the modern advantages of walkie-talkies and cross-country jeeps, success is not insured. The territory is wide and the wily prey instinctively keeps up-wind from its pursuers. Should a dog get too close when it has cornered a boar it is lucky if it lives to regret it. Local veterinarians are kept busy on the weekends stitching-up valuable hunting dogs. An average specimen of these bristly beasts weighs about 120 pounds/60 kilos but they can reach double those proportions. They also sport a menacing pair of fangs.

Traditionally, the innards and the head go to the hunter who brings down the prey. It will end up mounted on a wall. The rest of the spoils are skinned and divided among the team and will end up in family freezers. Eventually they will be prepared *alla cacciatora*, cooked the hunter's way, which varies from kitchen to kitchen but usually means stewed with onions, celery, carrots, tomatoes and herbs. Gastronomically the most desirable animal is a two year old

A hunter keeps in contact with teammates down the valley about the latest boar sightings.

with a reddish, salt and pepper coat. Older and tougher bears turn black — the infamous *bete noir*, and need long marinating in red wine and slow cooking before they can be made ready for the table. It is illegal to hunt the young who still have their light baby fur with dark bands running from head to tail.

The day of hunting concludes with a meal around the fire seasoned with many tales about the one that got away.

What beckons me back to the *Maremma* every winter is not the call of the wild and the hunting season but the rich aroma of game as it comes wafting from the kitchen of Da Michele Ai Due Cippi in the ancient hilltop town of Saturnia. I discovered this restaurant years ago when I was soaking off some winter growth in the hot sulphic pools of a spa that is providentially located in the valley just a few minutes away. Feeling the need for some serious nourishment after dieting for a couple of days on regulation food, I had sneaked up the hill to Da Michele, where I found that several tables were already occupied by persons I recognized as fellow inmates from down below.

Saturnia is a sleepy, pleasant place that maintains a leisurely pace even during the summer, when it seems mostly young married couples pushing baby prams stroll in the streets, enjoying an inexpensive holiday in its cool and refreshing atmosphere. In the valley below the situation is more hectic. Italian and foreign tourists in campers fight for parking space before they crowd under the waterfalls and into the ponds of mineral water created by the overflow from the source of the gushing springs a couple of kilometres up the road at the private spa.

I prefer Saturnia in the winter when the steam from the warm waters envelopes the cold valley floor and

Vapour from warm sulphuric waterfalls and pools rise from the cold valley floor beneath the town of Saturnia.

certainly choose as the first course for this wintry Sunday lunch, *acquacotta*, the traditional vegetable soup of the *Maremma*. Its name, which means 'cooked water', may be appropriate for Saturnia but does not give a clue to its goodness. Fundamentally it is *zuppa*, soup ladled over grilled (broiled) country-style bread. As is usual for a dish as basic as peasant soup, there exist as many variations of *acquacotta* in the Maremma as there are hilltop towns. Michele's is the richest, sweetest, most flavourful that I have come upon. Its principal ingredient is spinach flavoured with olive oil, onion, celery and tomato, seasoned with chilli pepper and simmered for a couple of hours before eggs blended with grated Parmesan cheese are added. Before it is served, another egg, one for each portion, is poached in the soup.

While you wait for your egg to poach, you can start with a beautiful *antipasto* plate called *filetti di caccia*, paper-thin slices of cured game meat, wild boar, deer, mountain goat, turkey and goose (I imagine these last two are of the farmyard variety), laid over a bed of rocket (arugula) and tomato. For those whose taste tends to the exotic, there is deer meat sausage, goose salami and *bresaola di cavallo*, cured raw fillet of horse meat served thinly sliced and dressed with a little olive oil, lemon juice and freshly ground black pepper. If you prefer, you can have an entire *antipasto* of cured wild boar composed of fillet, *prosciutto*, salami and sausage.

As a second course, wild boar comes out of the kitchen cooked in several different ways but the house speciality is *cinghiale al seme di finocchio*. Michele marinates a foreloin of young boar for twenty-four hours in red wine, rosemary, onion and garlic and cooks the chops to order in white wine and fennel

up in the town fires are blazing in the three dining rooms of Da Michele Ai Due Cippi. (The two *cippi* are inscribed Roman columns that stand in front of the restaurant and Michele Aniello is the proprietor.) While driving through the desolate, drizzly *Maremma*, I find it reassuring to remember that the four local women who cook for Michele are at that very moment making fresh pasta for *pappardelle*, wide noodles they will dress with wild boar sauce, and for *tortelli*, large ravioli they will stuff with puréed chestnuts seasoned with fennel seeds. Another will also be preparing dozens of *fregnacce*, a *Maremma* pancake (crêpe) filled with a variety of sauces, most typically a thick ragù.

When finally I arrive, however, I will almost

Sorano, one of several Etruscan hill
towns in the *Maremma* built on cliffs of
volcanic tufa.

Suckling pig ready to be roasted, capping one of the two inscribed Roman columns on the terrace of Da Michele Ai Due Cippi.

seeds. Since I have many opportunities closer to home to eat wild boar, when I travel to Saturnia I look forward to the delicacy of its domestic cousin, *maialino arrosto*, suckling pig roasted with bay, rosemary and white wine. When it comes to the table it is crackly on the outside and so tender on the inside that it practically dissolves on the fork.

From October to February, the *pièce de résistance* of Michele's menu is *germano al melograno*, roasted wild duck stuffed with ham and pomegranate seeds, seasoned with cloves and honey and basted with sherry. It is served with its succulent juices and decorated with more pomegranate seeds.

Even if you are not checked into the nearby 'fat farm' you will want to splurge with one of the rich desserts, thick cream puddings made with ricotta and mascarpone and topped with hot berry and chocolate sauces. A winter's meal that begins with *acquacotta* calls for an *acquavite* at the conclusion and Michele offers a fine selection of *grappa* that will brace you for a dip into the salubrious waters of Saturnia before heading for home.

Acquacotta

VEGETABLE SOUP WITH EGGS

The shepherds and charcoal burners of the Maremma kept a pot of water simmering over their fires and put whatever food they had at hand into this 'cooked water' soup. Michele Aniello's is an enriched version of the original and a winter's meal in itself. He serves it in individual soup terrines, with a slice of grilled (broiled) bread at the bottom, the soup ladled over it and a poached egg on top.

Serves 6.
3 celery stalks, finely chopped
1 large onion, finely chopped
1 small chilli, chopped
2fl oz/60ml (¼ cup) extra-virgin olive oil
1½lb/750g spinach, thick stalks (stems) removed
10oz/300g plum tomatoes, peeled and seeded
8 eggs
2tbsp/30ml freshly grated Parmesan cheese
6 slices firm, coarse-textured bread, grilled (broiled)
salt and pepper

Below: Maremma vegetable soup topped with a poached egg.

Gently sauté the celery, onion and chilli pepper in the oil until the onion is transparent but not browned. Add the spinach and stir until it has wilted and absorbed the flavours. Add the tomatoes, stir and leave to cook gently over low heat for about 30 minutes.

Stir in about 2½ pints/1.5 litres (1½ quarts) water and bring to the gentle boil. Leave to simmer for a further 60 minutes.

After 50 minutes, beat together 2 eggs with the Parmesan cheese. Stir the mixture into the soup. When the soup returns to the boil, break the remaining 6 eggs into the soup and cook until lightly poached.

Arrange the grilled (broiled) bread in soup bowls, ladle some soup in each bowl and top each with a poached egg.

Colombacci in Galera

PIGEONS 'IMPRISONED' IN A COVERED CASSEROLE

Colombacci, wood pigeons, scarce but still to be found in the Maremma, have dense, highly flavoured flesh. Domestic pigeons, squab, or rock cornish game can be substituted and the cooking time adjusted.

Serves 6.
3 pigeons, dressed
salt and pepper
3tbsp/45ml extra-virgin olive oil
1tsp/5ml tomato purée (paste)
6 cloves
8fl oz/250ml (1 cup) dry white wine
2fl oz/60ml (¼ cup) wine vinegar
1lb/3½oz/600g small onions

Wood pigeons cooked in a
covered casserole.

Germano al Melograno

— ROAST MALLARD DUCK WITH POMEGRANATES —

If you are unable to catch a mallard duck, try this recipe with any large game bird, even a domestic turkey. Pomegranates are a satisfying variant for cranberries.

Serves 6.
1 mallard duck, dressed
1 onion, finely chopped
1 tbsp/15ml extra-virgin olive oil
3oz/90g cooked ham, cut in julienne strips
2 tsp/10ml honey
4 cloves
2 pomegranates
salt and pepper
2fl oz/60ml dry sherry

Place the duck in a large flameproof casserole with enough cold water to cover. Bring to the boil over medium heat, then simmer for 5 minutes. Remove from the heat and leave to cool.

Meanwhile, prepare the stuffing. Fry the onion in the oil over low heat for about 5 minutes. Add the ham, honey, cloves and the seeds of 1 pomegranate. Season with salt and pepper to taste and cook for a further 2 minutes.

Dry the duck well and fill it with the stuffing. Close the opening with a skewer. Place the duck in a roasting pan and transfer to a pre-heated 400°F/200°C/Gas mark 6 oven. Brown the duck all over on top of the stove, then add the sherry and roast for about 60 minutes. Transfer the duck to a warm platter, pour over the cooking juices and garnish with the seeds from the second pomegranate.

Rub the pigeons with salt and pepper to taste. Pour the oil into a heavy based flameproof casserole just large enough to hold the pigeons with a tight-fitting lid. Heat the oil over medium heat, add the pigeons and brown them well all over.

Lower the heat and add tomato purée (paste), cloves, wine-vinegar and 8fl oz/250ml (1 cup) water. Stir well and add the onions. Cover the pan and cook over very low heat for about 1¼ hours, stirring occasionally.

Remove the pigeons and cut them in half lengthways. Arrange the halves on a warm serving dish, surround with the onions and coat with the cooking juices. Serve at once.

The lemon yellow blossoms of wild
rape and the first green on the vines
signal the arrival of spring in Tuscany.

SPRING

My first memory of early
spring in the Tuscan
countryside, dating back to
student days, is of women
with their children
wandering about the
hillsides stooping to gather
plants in their baskets.
When I was told they were
picking weeds to eat,
I remember thinking they
must be very poor indeed.
In truth I was the
impoverished one.

EDIBLE WEEDS, SPRING GREENS & AROMATIC VINEGARS

My first memory of early spring in the Tuscan countryside, dating back to student days, is of women with their children wandering about the hillsides stooping to gather plants in their baskets. When I was told they were picking weeds to eat, I remember thinking they must be very poor, indeed. In truth, I was the impoverished one. I had never heard of an edible weed, let alone eaten one. It must have been shortly afterwards that I tried my first leaf of *rucola selvatica*, wild rocket (arugula), and was immediately hooked on its spicy, nutty, mustard-flavoured taste — a far cry from the bland Iceberg lettuce I had been raised on.

That was just the beginning. I soon discovered there were dozens of different edible weeds far tastier than anything found in the market which mother nature provides precisely during that period before spring has settled in, when nothing green and tender grows in your garden. As those old Tuscan women and their contemporary counterparts, diminishing in number but still to be seen searching the fields, know, these plants also have specific beneficial properties for combatting the grippes and various other ill humours of that dank season.

I had my first lesson in edible weeds from an American neighbour who has lived here forever. Barbara learned about these plants from the locals and by following her own New England pioneering instincts. Now she gives field-trip lessons to the village children on the subject.

When Barbara sets out on a walk to gather weeds for a salad of wild greens, she searches for a variety of different tastes and textures. Into a basket will go some of the serrated, oval leaves of *salvastrella* (salad burnet) that have a slight cucumber taste. She will have to hunt for some *raperonzolo* (rampion), now almost extinct in our area. Both its tender green leaves and crisp white roots can be eaten raw. She prefers *crescione dei prati* (bittercress) to watercress, which it resembles in taste but with more firmness to the bite. Growing out of old dry-stone walls can be found flat, greyish green rosettes of *terracrepolo*, often called wall salad. Barbara avoids the more bitter greens in her selection, but for me, the more bitter the better, so I would add some dandelion leaves and the tender shoots of wild chicory to this salad.

Other weeds need to be cooked before being eaten. *Castrabecco* (wild salsify), sometimes referred to as goat's beard because of its stringy white seed filaments, has a slightly twisted root not unlike a parsnip. When it is boiled it tastes subtly similar to artichoke heart. Barbara makes delicious ravioli stuffed with *strigoli* (bladdercampion) instead of spinach. She calculates that it takes about 100 of its tender tops for one portion of ravioli. Weed-gatherers are not clock watchers. Even those for whom time is money may want to consider spending a couple of hours gathering *asparagini*, wild asparagus, given the market price of their cultivated cousins. Their thin green spears are very aromatic and strongly flavoured, and their tender tips are delicious in a risotto or in a *frittata*, an Italian omelette.

Another food that is gathered from the Tuscan countryside during early spring is the common land snail that the Tuscans call *lumaca*, pronounced with their characteristic lightly aspirated 'c' — lu-ma-ha. Snails are collected at night after an April shower when they sneak out of the recesses in stone walls where they have spent the winter to feed on the grassy banks of road-side ditches.

Baskets of edible weeds at market.

This seems to be a diversion primarily for father and son, though not everywhere in Tuscany. Most citizens of Chianti would not stoop to pick up a snail but on the bordering areas of the Valdarno and the Casentino it is a popular pastime. Late one night when I had dropped off a friend outside her house, I heard a cry of alarm. She had practically stumbled over a man crawling along her garden wall with a plastic bag and a flashlight. Fortunately it was not a burglar making off with the silver but a neighbour hot on the trail of some particularly promising snails.

In outward appearance these Tuscan gastropods seem poor country cousins to the aristocratic *escargot* from Burgundy. Though they have small bodies in undistinguished brownish shells, their fruity and firm flesh is savoured as a rustic delicacy by devotees. Every spring in Cavriglia, a small town above the Valdarno, enthusiasts celebrate the *Sagra delle Lumache*, a gastronomic feast in honour of the snail.

Days before the feast the women begin to prepare the feted food by the thousands for the featured dish, *lumache al sugo*, snails in sauce. Forty per person is considered a fair portion for the first helping. Before the snails can be cooked, however, they have to be purged. For five days they are kept in large containers of water to which salt, vinegar, and a dusting of bran have been added along with a firmly attached lid, preferably with a large stone set on top. (I am told the leverage power of hundreds of hungry snails is amazing.) Everyday they are washed and their bath water changed. At the end of the purgation period they are blanched for five minutes in boiling water, a few lots at a time.

Next comes the part that takes real dedication. Each snail is removed from its shell by means of a toothpick. The shell is thoroughly washed and the body is boiled for one hour in water and vinegar. Then the two parts are re-assembled. Finally the snails are cooked in a thick tomato sauce seasoned with olive oil, *prosciutto*, carrot, onion, parsley and chilli pepper. Well might you wonder whether it was worth all that trouble. Judging from the heaps of empty shells on every table that grow before your very eyes and the blissful expression of the eater as they suck each one clean, the answer is apparent. I can vouch for the sauce.

Whereas Tuscans might go heavy on the sauce with their snails, they use a light touch when it comes to seasoning their greens — salt, extra-virgin olive oil and red wine vinegar, nothing else. I have heard them say, with characteristic sardonic humour, that anyone who uses anything more (i.e. the French) does so to disguise the taste of their inferior olive oil. The rule-of-thumb recipe calls for plenty of salt, a generous amount of oil and just a little vinegar (the proportion is usually four to one but will depend on the greens), not necessarily in that order. I know a celebrated cook

Bunches of wild and cultivated asparagus.

Terracotta rooftops of the medieval hill hamlet of Volpaia, near Radda in Chianti.

towns of Gaiole, Radda and Castellina, the historic heart of Chianti.

The hamlet's some thirty inhabitants share its old stone buildings on narrow streets and two small piazzas with the best of contemporary wine-making equipment, including huge stainless-steel fermentation tanks that had to be lowered through the roof of what was once a medieval chapel. Elegant oak ageing vats are now housed in the vast crypt that descends beneath the former Renaissance church, whose splendid nave and apse are transformed every year into a gallery for exhibitions of avant-garde Italian art that attracts international attention.

These creative innovations which have infused vitality and prosperity into this solitary jewel of the Tuscan countryside that could have deteriorated into a ghost town or, worse yet, a 'holiday village', are the work of the energetic young couple who own Valpaia, Giovannella Stianti and Carlo Mascheroni. Giovannella's father, a Florentine industrialist, bought the property in 1967, and presented it to her as a wedding gift.

Almost ten years ago Giovannella and Carlo decided to revive another traditional craft at Volpaia, the artisan production of fine wine vinegars. Formerly every winery, large and small, made vinegar, which is, as the French say, only wine gone sour. When fermented grape juice is exposed to the air for a long enough time, bacteria forms on top and the wine turns to vinegar. Because winemakers fight against bacteria and the making of vinegar encourages its growth, the Italian laws regulating both processes became stricter and wineries stopped making vinegar altogether. Now Volpaia is the only winery in Tuscany that also has the licence to produce vinegar.

who first dissolves the salt in the vinegar and then adds the oil.

In Tuscany it is easy to come by excellent olive oil. Fine wine vinegar is more difficult to find. I must drive almost an hour to the hamlet of Volpaia to obtain the region's best, but it is well worth the trip. It is a unique place that merits a periodical visit even apart from purchasing its exceptional vinegars.

Volpaia sits high on an incline at 2000 feet/608 metres, above steep slopes planted with vineyards and olive groves which produce the estate's premium wines and oil. From here you can enjoy a stunning view of the wooded hills that surround the ancient

Like fine wine Volpaia vinegars are aged in wood and carefully controlled.

compatible tastes, balancing flavours, eliminating aromas that overwhelmed others. Periodically an informal panel, composed of winemaker, herbalist, family cook, a friend or two who happened to be around at the time and the two young technicians they had hired to oversee the entire project, would meet to taste and critique the preliminary results. (Wine and olive oil tasters spit and might cleanse their palates with a morsel of bread. Vinegar tasters try to keep their taste buds open by sucking it out of sugar cubes that neutralize the high acidic content.)

Finally, they concocted five different recipes. The first three use red wine vinegar as a base and the other two are made with white. Like some expensive perfumes each fragrance is numbered. '1' is called *Erbe*, herbs, and is a blend of fennel, juniper, rosemary, thyme, balm, bay, garlic and chilli pepper. Number '2', *Spezie*, spices, combines cloves, nutmeg and black pepper with several herbs to temper the taste. The third, *Orto*, vegetable garden, features parsley, celery, onion and garlic, basic flavours to many Italian dishes. '4' *Fiori*, flowers, is a white wine vinegar aromatized with a pot pourri of antique rose, marigold, borage, lavender, elder, bitter orange, clary and sage. Number '5' *Fresco*, fresh, also has a white wine vinegar base and tastes of cool peppermint and green anise. Each of these five bouquets of mixed aromas are put into large linen sacks and then left to macerate in their base vinegar for about two months.

The method Volpaia uses to make the vinegar itself is a process as carefully controlled as wine making. To make fine vinegar you must begin with good quality wine. This wine slowly percolates into a tank through three tiers of stainless-steel baskets loosely filled with wood shavings and dried vine

When Giovanella and Carlo had made the decision to restore vinegar making at Volpaia they came up with a unique idea. Besides the classic red and white wine vinegars, they would *not* produce the usual aromatized varieties using a single herb like tarragon or basil, but ones flavoured with bouquets of different aromas. They began with a selection of some seventy different aromas culled from the garden greens, herbs and flowers on the estate, as well as more exotic spices, macerating each single aroma in both white and red vinegar.

Then began a two-year period of painstaking experimentation during which they tested various blends. It was a process of trial and error, discovering

Flowers and spices as well as herbs
and vegetables are blended and put
into linen sacks, then left to macerate
in the vinegar.

(grape) cuttings. These allow the wine to oxidize and provide a support for the bacteria. This method, which takes about two weeks, preserves the aroma and flavour of the wine, whereas industrially produced vinegar, which can be made in a day, smells and tastes mostly of acetic acid.

Volpaia red wine vinegar, like fine wine is aged up to a year in large chestnut vats and then in small oak barrels (the white ages about a month in larch wood), which confers body to its structure and refines the taste. The result is a vinegar with a clear, clean colour and fresh aroma that is smooth on the palate with a pleasant acidic bite.

The maceration of the aromas confers a complexity to these condiments that give them an almost alchemistic effect and unlimited possibilities in the kitchen. I have tried them with success on everything from salads and fish to fruit and ice cream.

Many of the aromas that flavour Volpaia's fine vinegars are grown on the estate.

Barbara Giuffrida's Edible Weeds, Wild Greens and Flower Salad

The tastiness of a wild greens salad depends on their variety. All of these are commonly found so you should be able to gather several of them at least. A handful of dandelion leaves and chicory can be added if you like the taste of bitter greens. Barbara also recommends a teaspoon of finely chopped nettle leaves, which lose their sting when cut up and are, she says, 'very good for you'.

Serves 6.
1 clove garlic
salt
red wine vinegar
extra-virgin olive oil
A GENEROUS HANDFUL OF EACH OF THE FOLLOWING:
White mustard (*Sinapis alba*)
Hairy bittercress (*cardamine hirsuta*)
Hedge garlic (*alliaria petiolate*)
Common winter cress (*Barbarea vulgaris*)
Salad burnet (*Poterium sanguisorba*)
Brooklime (*veronica beccabunga*)
Corn salad (*Valerianella locusta*)
Sow thistle (*sonchus arvensis*)
violets, wild marigolds and borage flowers to garnish

Rub the salad bowl with garlic. To make the dressing, dissolve the salt in vinegar.

Add 1 part red wine vinegar to 3 or 4 parts extra-virgin olive oil and beat together. Spoon over the mixed greens and toss together until all the leaves are lightly coated. Serve at once.

Zucchini a Scapece

COURGETTES (ZUCCHINI) MARINATED IN OLIVE OIL
WITH RED WINE VINEGAR

Nuccia, the cook at Volpaia, is an institution. These are two of her recipes that feature the estate's fine wine vinegars. For marinating these courgettes (zucchini) she suggests using *Orto*, their aromatic red wine vinegar with flavours from the vegetable garden.

Serves 4–6.
1½ lb/750g small, firm zucchini
4fl oz/125ml (½ cup) extra-virgin olive oil
salt and pepper
3½fl oz/100ml (scant ½ cup) good quality red wine vinegar
½tsp/2.5ml dried oregano
2 cloves garlic, finely chopped

Soak the courgettes (zucchini) in cold water for 15 minutes. Drain and slice as thinly as possible.

Heat the oil in a large heavy-based frying pan (skillet). Add the courgettes, season with salt and pepper. Turning frequently, fry over medium high heat until slices are light brown and tender: cooking time varies from 5–10 minutes, depending on the quality of the courgettes. Remove the zucchini with a slotted spoon and spread out on absorbent kitchen paper to drain.

Add the vinegar to the pan and stir rapidly over high heat for about 30 seconds. Pour the contents of the pan over the courgettes, sprinkle with oregano and garlic. Check the seasoning, cover the dish and leave to marinate for several hours. Serve at room temperature.

Melanzane e Giardiniera

FRIED AUBERGINE (EGGPLANT) AND MIXED VEGETABLES
SEASONED WITH WHITE WINE VINEGAR

Nuccia recommends using Volpaia's *Fresco* aromatic white wine vinegar with this perfect dish for a late springtime luncheon. This may be served either hot or at room temperature.

Serves 4–6.
6fl oz/180ml (¾ cup) extra-virgin olive oil
1 large or 2 small aubergines (eggplants), diced
1 onion, sliced
2 celery stalks, sliced
2 carrots, peeled and sliced
5oz/150g stoned (pitted) green olives
6 plum tomatoes, peeled and chopped
salt and pepper
1tbsp/15ml capers, well drained
1tbsp/15ml pine nuts
4fl oz/125ml (½ cup) good white vinegar

Heat 4fl oz/125ml (½ cup) oil in a large heavy-based frying pan (skillet). Add the aubergine (eggplant) and fry over medium heat until golden. Remove with a slotted spoon and drain on absorbent kitchen paper.

Add the remaining oil to the pan and, when hot, the onion, celery, carrots, olives and tomatoes. Season with salt and pepper and, stirring occasionally, cook over medium heat for about 10 minutes.

Stir in the capers, pine nuts and vinegar. Cook for a further 5 minutes. Remove from the heat and allow to cool slightly, then stir in the aubergine (eggplant) and adjust the seasoning.

Perhaps no experience in a Tuscan restaurant is quite so irritating and frustrating and, unfortunately, common, than to be served a salad of *lattuga*, common lettuce, and vegetables from a can, especially when you have just seen heaps of tasty greens and piles of lustrous vegetables in the nearby market. If truth be told, most Tuscan restaurateurs, proud of their delicious soups and roasted meats, tend to give greens short shrift.

There are, of course, exceptions, and Carlo Cioni, proprietor of Da Delfina, a country restaurant about 20 miles/32 kilometres west of Florence in the direction of Pistoia and the Montalbano hills, is, perhaps, the most notable. Carlo inherited his respect for greens and vegetables from his mother, Delfina, now in her mid-eighties, who still presides over her kitchen. She began cooking for guests fifty years ago, first for the hunters who came to shoot on the huge game reserve that surrounds the Villa of Artimino, originally built as a hunting lodge for Ferdinando de' Medici in the late sixteenth century. Then she cooked for the weekend tourists who came to see the villa. In 1975, she opened her own restaurant just a couple kilometres up the road below the medieval walled village of Artimino.

Not long after then, I was treated to my first meal at Da Delfina by Florentine friends who considered it a find best kept secret. Word soon spread, however,

and it has long been the favourite destination of citizens from the Tuscan capital who want to combine a trip into the countryside with an excellent Sunday dinner and maybe bring back some bottles of Carmignano, the area's fine red wine that was a favourite of the Medici. I know a chef who drives out from the city just to eat a plate of pig's liver. He claims it is the best in all of Tuscany.

My thoughts turn towards Artimino in spring when the days are warm enough to enjoy lunch on the terrace surrounded by vineyards and villas and wooded hills and I long to taste the fresh abundance of the season. I know that when I arrive and take a look beyond the rustic open grill at the entrance of the kitchen into the large work space behind, I will see a team of young cooks tieing the trimmed spears of asparagus into bundles, removing the pistils from bright yellow courgette (zucchini) flowers (perhaps the most cheerful sign of spring in the Italian kitchen), shelling broad (fava) beans, cleaning artichokes, cutting the tender tops of nettles, plucking the flowers from borage, and often Delfina herself, podding small, sweet peas.

This spring bounty will be prepared in a dozen different ways but happily it can also be enjoyed all at the same time. In a superb dish Carlo Cioni calls *fritto misto alla fiorentina*, a Florentine mixed fry, the ingredients are dipped into a light batter and quickly fried in olive oil. He usually includes little pieces of meat cooked in the same way. Should you crave a totally vegetarian feast, Signor Cioni will add an array of edible weeds, wild herbs, flowers, greens and vegetables gathered from his kitchen garden, restaurant courtyard, surrounding fields and even from the neighbour's back garden.

Signora Delfina began cooking for guests at Artimino over fifty years ago and still presides over her restaurant's kitchen.

A carpet of spring green covers the
Montalbano hills west of Florence.

Stufato di Baccelli

—— STEWED BROAD (FAVA) BEANS ——

The traditional way to enjoy fresh broad (fava) beans is right out of their shells, raw, with a piece of *pecorino* cheese and a glass of white wine. Carlo Cioni serves this dish late in the season when the beans are less tender.

Serves 4–6.
1tbsp/15ml extra-virgin olive oil
1 clove garlic, finely chopped
1 onion, finely chopped
1tbsp/15ml finely chopped fresh rosemary
4oz/125g unsalted bacon (slab bacon), diced
1lb/500g plum tomatoes, peeled and seeded
1½lb/750g shelled broad (fava) beans
salt and pepper

Heat the oil in a medium saucepan. Add the garlic, onion and rosemary. Sauté gently until the onion is transparent. Add the bacon and continue to cook over low heat until most of the fat has melted. Add the tomatoes and stir well. Add the beans, cover and simmer over gentle heat for about 20 minutes, or until the beans are tender. Adjust the seasoning and serve.

Frittata di Asparagi

—— ASPARAGUS OMELETTE ——

If you dine *da Delfina* in early spring you may be lucky enough to have your *frittata* made with wild asparagus. Any tender asparagus tips will do nicely.

Serves 6.
3lb/1.5kg asparagus
3tbsp/45ml extra-virgin olive oil
4 cloves garlic, halved
8 eggs
4tbsp/60ml freshly grated Parmesan cheese
salt and pepper

Break the tough ends off the asparagus, then blanch the stalks in boiling salted water for about 6 minutes. Drain the asparagus and cut into pieces about 2in/5cm long.

Heat the oil in a round 8in/20cm ovenproof pan over medium heat. Add the garlic and cook until just golden. Remove the garlic and discard.

In a bowl, lightly beat the eggs with the Parmesan and salt and pepper to taste.

Arrange the asparagus in the pan, pour the eggs on top and stir so the asparagus is well distributed. Transfer to a preheated 350°F/180°C/Gas mark 4 oven and bake for about 10 minutes, until the *frittata* is set. Turn the *frittata* out into a plate and serve hot.

Stewed broad (fava) beans.

Fritto Misto alla Fiorentina
— FLORENTINE MEAT AND VEGETABLE MIXED-FRY —

Perhaps Delfina calls this dish 'Florentine' because so many of them drive out from the city to her restaurant to enjoy it. It can be made with or without the meat. For the vegetarian version she might add slices of tomatoes, sage leaves, aubergine (egg plant) fennel or any number of other greens and vegetables growing in her garden.

Serves 6.
2 glove artichokes, tough outer leaves and spikes
removed
juice of 1 lemon
7½oz/225g (1¾ cups) plain (all-purpose) flour
2 eggs, lightly beaten
2tbsp/30ml dry fine bread crumbs
1¾ pints/1 litre (1 quart) extra-virgin olive oil
5oz/150g skinless chicken, cut in small pieces
5oz/150g skinless rabbit, cut in small pieces
3½oz/100g brains, in small pieces
5oz/150g lamb cutlets
2 small courgettes (zucchini), cut into small strips
6 courgettes (zucchini) flowers, when available, stalks
(stems) and pistols removed
a few borage or malva leaves, if available

Cut the zucchini into short strips. Remove the tough outer leaves and spikes from the artichokes.

Cut the artichokes into wedges and drop into a bowl of water with lemon juice to prevent discoloration. Set aside.

Slowly sift 3½oz/100g (¾ cup) flour into 10fl oz/300ml (1¼ cups) water and beat well with a wooden spoon until smooth. Arrange the remaining flour, eggs and bread crumbs on three separate plates.

Heat half the olive oil in a deep frying pan (skillet). Dredge the pieces of chicken, rabbit, lamb cutlets and brain in the flour, then dip them into the beaten egg. Coat with bread crumbs. Fry in the hot oil until golden. Remove with a slotted spoon and drain on absorbent kitchen paper.

In another deep frying pan (skillet), heat the remaining olive oil. Dip the vegetables including the zucchini flowers into the batter very quickly, then fry in the clean oil until golden brown. Drain on kitchen paper. Serve together with the meat.

Delfina's 'Florentine' mixed vegetable and meat fry.

SHEEP'S MILK CHEESE

Marzolino, little March, is the pretty Tuscan name for the season's first and most esteemed batch of sheep's milk cheese. In Italian *pecora* means sheep and *pecorino*, sheep's milk cheese. Besides *pecorino toscano* there is the better-known and exported *pecorino romano*, a slightly oily, hard cheese used for grating, and the piquant *pecorino siciliano*, which is sometimes coloured with saffron or seasoned with peppercorns. These *pecorino* cheeses are all made in more or less the same way. The difference is due to what goes into the sheep. Because the grass is always greener in Tuscany, or so it seems to Tuscans, *pecorino toscano* boasts a taste that is uniquely sweet and delicate. And since the herbage is freshest and most fragrant in March, *marzolino* is the best sheep's milk cheese you can find.

I have the good luck to be able to get mine close to home, made by my neighbour, Signora Nella Anichini. She and her husband, Carlo, and their five children are one of the few families in the area who work their own small farm. For centuries the land in this part of Tuscany was owned by a few aristocratic families and share-cropped by tenant farmers. After the world wars the peasants began to leave the land for town and salaried jobs. Carlo remained and finally managed to buy his farm. It is called *Le Selve*, The Woods, and the house, set high on a wooded knoll, enjoys a 360-degree view of the valleys of Gaiole and Radda in Chianti. Today Carlo and Nella, with the help of the children who live and work in town, tend their own vineyards, olive groves, woods and, of course, sheep.

Their flock now numbers only twenty or so, and I get the feeling these are kept solely because of the pleasure Nella clearly derives from milking and making cheese. During the height of the season, from March through June, the ewes produce about 35 pints/ 20 litres (20 quarts) of milk daily, enough to make four beautiful forms of *pecorino*, each weighing about 2 pounds/1kg, plus a mound of rich ricotta. They continue to give milk in decreasing amounts into early autumn and by September her cheese production is down to two then one form a day.

In the spring Nella makes cheese twice every day, in the early morning and evening following each of the day's two milkings. Over the years I have watched her at work innumerable times and occasionally I have brought along a friend or two. At first she seemed surprised that visitors from afar might be interested but she proceeded as if we were not even there, completely absorbed in her task. The only day we had to wait was when I arrived at a critical moment during her favourite TV programme, *Il Fuoco dell'Amore*, (The Flame of Love), the Italian title for the American soap opera, The Young and the Restless.

Nella's art of cheesemaking is simplicity itself. First she pours the still warm milk into a large pan and sets it on the kitchen table. Next she performs a little herbal magic. Someone discovered a long time ago that the enzymes found on the stamens of the wild artichoke plant flower act as a rennet. They curdle milk. These plants, called *pressuria*, grow along the dry stone terraces of Nella's garden and every July she picks about fifty of their gorgeous royal blue flowers, dries the heads and plucks out enough stamens to last until the following year.

After soaking a pinch of these stamens in a cup of water for about ten minutes she removes them and

A perfect combination, *pecorino* cheese and a slice of pear. (Painted still life, Green Apples In A Bowl by Jacques Feger.)

In Tuscany the grass is always greener and the milk from these sheep makes Italy's best *pecorino* cheese.

local shepherd. When it is offered to me in a restaurant, I take it as a sure sign that I am in the right place. The proprietor has made an effort to provide his clients a delicacy.

Signora Anichini does not usually make *raviggiolo*, except on special request from family or friends. When the milk has coagulated, she carries it into the pantry, the inner sanctum of her farmhouse, a marvellous little room pungent with the aroma of cheese. In autumn it is a real Aladdin's cave. The shelves are filled with jars of artichoke hearts under oil and tomato preserves. Carlo has supended bunches of white *malvasia* grapes from a rod to dry for his Vin Santo. From the banisters of a stairway leading to the attic one of their sons, a butcher, has attached strings of salami and a whole *prosciutto* to air. Most amazing of all, hanging from the topmost beams in a corner of the ceiling, next to an incongruous coloured glass chandelier, are large bunches of small cherry tomatoes still attached to their stems. These tomatoes will remain fresh all through the winter, providing Nella with a supply for her kitchen.

Now she is ready for the actual preparation of the cheese. She extracts the lumps of curd from the pan with her fingers and transfers them to an oval-shaped terracotta bowl. As she does this she breaks up the lumps in the bowl by pinching them to eliminate any air holes. When all the curds have been collected in the bowl, she begins to massage them gently, slightly cupping her hands. In what I can only describe as a state of meditation she continuously kneads and turns the curds inside the form for about fifteen minutes, pouring the remaining whey that is released by this action back into the milk pan, until her experienced hands tell her the curds have become perfectly

pours the remaining brownish coloured liquid into the milk. She stirs the milk to make sure the rennet gets to the bottom, covers the pan and waits for about a half hour, depending on the heat of the day. By then the curds have formed.

At this point some cheesemakers lift the curds from the whey forming a fresh cheese called *raviggiolo*, which is pressed into little moulds and eaten for breakfast or served as an *antipasto*, seasoned with pepper and garnished with herbs and wild lettuces. It has the shimmery texture of yogurt, a delicate taste and must be enjoyed at its very freshest. When the curds are used for *raviggiolo*, it means, of course, there is nothing left to make *pecorino*. This makes it difficult to come-by unless you are on good terms with your

compact. Finished, she rubs the cheese with ordinary table salt to draw out more moisture and impart savour.

During the next twenty-four hours the cheese will rest in its terracotta bowl and release a bit more liquid. Then she hangs it along side the others in a long, narrow, white cotton hammock tied to a rod suspended between two chairs in her pantry. This simple system allows the cheeses to dry evenly without developing mould. After about a week they are ready for the table.

Pecorino toscano can be eaten 'young' at the age of a week or so; 'medium', at the age of about three months and 'aged', at around nine months. When it is fresh, it has a milky colour and aroma, a soft, creamy texture (*pastoso*, doughy, is how Nella describes it), and a delicate taste. With age the cheese becomes harder and the taste sharper. When Tuscans buy *pecorino*, they ask for one that is more or less *piccante*, piquant.

When the cheeses are a week old, Signora Anichini destines some for long ageing. She selects ones that have not developed any cracks, rubs them with a paste made of flour and olive oil and stores them in a large terracotta jar under her work table. Around Christmas time they will go to the few fortunates who have reserved them long in advance. She sells her fresh cheese to neighbours like me who are regular customers and to a shopkeeper who comes from the Arno Valley, almost an hour's drive from the farm, to buy as many as are available. I find it reassuring when a merchant will drive that distance to provide his clients with such special cheese.

There is another source for quality *pecorino*, more massed produced. In the large sheep raising areas of Tuscany, Il Mugello, on the region's north eastern boundry bordering the Apennine mountains, and in the Maremma, a coastal plain south west of Siena, where flocks number several hundred, shepherds use a faster method to make their cheese. The curds are pressed rather than kneaded into large, wide, circular forms with perforated bottoms. This allows the litres of whey to run out and collect in a large container placed beneath the working surface. *Pecorino* made this way comes out thick and round in form and will weigh at least twice as much as Signora Anichini's traditionally cylindrical shaped *marzolino*. In shops these larger cheeses are usually sold by the wedge. Those who raise sheep exclusively for slaughter sell the milk to large cheese factories. At this point

Nella Anichini massages the curds of her sheep's milk in a ceramic bowl forming them into the characteristic *marzolino* shape.

industrial methods take over and cow's milk, which is cheaper and more plentiful, is often added to the sheep's milk.

Signora Anichini's cheese-making session is not yet over. In a way the best is yet to come. She brings the pan of whey back to the kitchen and heats it on her stove. When it reaches the boiling point the remaining fat protein in the liquid coagulates and rises to the surface. Lo and behold, we have ricotta. With a large spoon she lifts the ricotta out of the pan and transfers it into a perforated mould. In one of those satisfying gestures that completes a perfect agricultural cycle, the liquid that remains after the ricotta forms is fed back to her sheep. Nella told me that during the war, when food was scarce, even this liquid was a valuable source of nutrition. She kept it for her family to pour over their bread.

Tuscan *pecorino* is a table cheese, too precious to be used in cooking or grated over food. I have three favourite ways to enjoy it. The simplest and most classic is a wedge of seasoned *pecorino* eaten with the perfect pear. This is one of those ideal marriages between contrasting, yet complementary, textures and tastes, the juicy, sweet pear and the somewhat dry, piquant *pecorino*.

The other two I picked up from Piero Stucchi-

Prinetti, owner of Badia a Coltibuono vineyard, during the many work-day meals we used to put together. His wife, Lorenza de'Medici, is more famous for her cuisine but he has a few tricks of his own. Both dishes each feature a fine product from that estate, extra-virgin olive oil and mountain flower honey.

Cut yourself a healthy slice of medium-aged *pecorino*, douse it with the very best extra-virgin olive oil and add a few twists of freshly ground black pepper. With a fresh green salad and some country-style bread this makes a completely satisfying light meal.

The next one was probably brought to Tuscany by the many Sardinian shepherds who have immigrated here and are largely responsible for our high-quality *pecorino*. It is an uncomplicated version of their regional speciality, *sebadas*, deep-fried cheese discs with honey. Grill (broil) a slice of young *pecorino* until a bubbly crust has formed on the outside and top it with a strong-flavoured flower or herbal honey. Warm cheese and honey may sound like strange bedfellows but they combine to make a very tasty wintry afternoon snack or dessert.

The Anichini like the taste of a bite of fresh garlic from their garden with a piece of young *pecorino*. They eat ricotta with a little sugar for breakfast and as a dessert with bits of chocolate and some of Carlo's excellent Vin Santo mixed in. It is also the featured ingredient in several traditional Tuscan recipes.

Not far from where Nella Anichini makes ricotta another remarkable woman, Miranda Minucci, uses it in the kitchen of her restaurant to fill large, luscious, freshly made ravioli. Miranda, as she is known to all, is a character. Chaucer could have encountered her on

The bunches of cherry tomatoes still attached to their stems hanging from the ceiling of Signora Anichini's well laden larder will remain fresh all through the winter.

'La' Miranda stretches the fresh egg
pasta that she will fill with ricotta and
spinach and fold to form her
celebrated ravioli.

his way to Canterbury and certainly Moliere and Goldoni had her in mind in several of their comedies. Her establishment came into existence over 150 years ago as an *osteria*, a roadside inn where weary travellers could change horses, have a hot meal and bed-down for the night. There was one large dormitory for the men, another for the women and a room apart for nuns on the go. There are still rooms upstairs and across the way Miranda has built a smart new edifice. Now travellers drive up in Alfas and BMWs.

The times may have changed but Miranda has not. She is one of the last of a disappearing breed of purveyors of food and lodging. Along with the proverbial craftiness of the innkeeper, she also has that once traditional but now rare willingness to go out of the way to satisfy her clients. No matter how full her restaurant, she always seems to find space for the hungry traveller, even if it is a seat at the family table. On a cold and rainy winter evening when most of her colleagues have long called it a night and retired to the TV, Miranda will stir the embers of her large kitchen fire and find something to put on the grill. Have a friend from afar who is longing for fried courgette (zucchini) blossoms? Phone Miranda and minutes later she will have them on the table. Feel a little peckish in the wee hours, drop by and she will hustle up a bowl of spaghetti.

Miranda has her off days but when she is good, she is very good, indeed. In any case she rolls out the best fresh ravioli stuffed with spinach and ricotta that I have ever come across and there is a lot of competition around. It is practically a staple in these parts. Miranda serves hers simply sautéed in butter seasoned with fresh sage or topped with a sauce of tomatoes and basil. Either way they are memorable.

Ravioli con Spinaci e Ricotta
SPINACH AND RICOTTA RAVIOLI
WITH TOMATO SAUCE

Cow's milk ricotta can be used as a substitute for sheep's milk ricotta. In Tuscany spinach and ricotta ravioli are often served simply dressed with butter and fresh sage leaves.

Serves 6.

SAUCE:
4fl oz/125ml (½ cup) extra-virgin olive oil
1 celery stalk, finely chopped
1 small carrot, peeled and finely chopped
1 small onion, finely chopped
3 cloves garlic, finely chopped
2lb/1kg ripe plum tomatoes, peeled and chopped, or canned Italian tomatoes, drained and chopped
12 fresh basil leaves
salt and pepper
2tbsp/30ml unsalted butter, to serve

RAVIOLI:
1¾lb/900g fresh spinach, cooked and well drained
10oz/300g ricotta cheese
2 egg yolks
4oz/125g fresh Parmesan cheese, finely grated
12oz/350g freshly made egg pasta
flour
salt and pepper

To make the sauce, heat the olive oil over low heat in a saucepan. Add the celery, carrot, onion and garlic. Sauté gently, stirring occasionally, about 4 minutes, until transparent. Add the tomatoes and basil. Season with salt and pepper to taste. Stir well, partly cover and simmer very gently, about 45 minutes, until the liquid has evaporated.

Spinach and ricotta ravioli are traditionally sautéed in butter and sage or topped with fresh tomato sauce.

along the edges and around the stuffing. Use a pastry wheel with a fluted edge and cut the pasta into 2in/5cm squares.

Bring a large pan of salted water to the boil. Add the ravioli and cook about 2 minutes, until they rise to the surface. Drain the pasta well and arrange on a warm serving dish. Toss with the butter and coat with the tomato sauce. Serve piping hot.

Cremino di Ricotta con Lamponi
—— CREAMED RICOTTA WITH RASPBERRY PUREÉ ——

This recipe is from La Bottega del 30 in the little village of Villa a Sesta, not far from Siena. The topping changes with the season. In winter it is served with a chocolate sauce.

1 vanilla pod (bean)
8fl oz/250ml (1 cup) milk
7oz/200g (1 cup) granulated sugar
1lb 3oz/600g fresh ricotta cheese
2lb/1kg fresh raspberries
3½oz/100g (½ cup) caster (superfine) sugar
mixed berries for decoration

Soak the vanilla pod (bean) in the milk for at least 30 minutes.

Gradually add the vanilla-flavoured milk and granulated sugar to the ricotta, beating constantly until the mixture is smooth.

Push the raspberries through a sieve (strainer) and discard the seeds. Sweeten the raspberries with caster sugar to taste. Divide the beaten ricotta between 6 dessert glasses. Top with the raspberry purée and decorate with berries. Serve chilled but not too cold.

Meanwhile, to make the filling, squeeze any excess water out of the spinach. Chop the spinach very finely and combine it with the ricotta cheese, egg yolks and Parmesan. Stir well with a fork until well blended. Set aside.

On a lightly floured surface, roll out the pasta until very thin. Cut into strips about 2½in/6cm wide and 12in/30cm long. Place small mounds of the spinach mixture on half the strips; they should be placed at intervals of about 2½in/6cm apart. Brush the edges of the pasta between the mounds with cold water. Cover the strips with the unfilled pasta and seal by pressing

EASTER CHOCOLATES & PASCHAL LAMB

In my neck of the Tuscan woods there grows a scrubby kind of European white oak called, *cerro*, that proliferates in this rocky soil. In autumn the leaves turn a bright copper and remain on their branches throughout the winter, adding welcome patches of vibrant colour to an otherwise bleak landscape. On a clear February afternoon, when the setting sun catches them in its rays, the hills seem aflame. By March the leaves begin to look sad and straggly but they still hang on, the last vestige of winter. Just when you think they will never go, a late March storm blows them away and almost overnight these oaks begin to shoot forth their spring green. *Pasqua*, the Paschal season, that celebrates another kind of passage from death to new life, is here.

Easter is still an important religious and family feastday in Italy. Easter Monday is a national holiday (no longer Easter Tuesday, unfortunately) and the arrival of the first vacationing friends and tourists, usually sun-seekers from the North, adds to the festive atmosphere. You may happen upon another sign of the season, a curious sight along city streets and country lanes: the local parish priest vested in black cassock and white linen surplice accompanied by a tiny acolyte or two making the rounds of the parish for the annual blessing of the home. He carries a container with holy water and an aspergill and the boy holds a bag for the expected donation. The visit of the priest is the occasion for spring cleaning, and the mistress of the house will have prepared fresh eggs and bread to be blessed. This custom has its origin in bygone days when the 'black fast', abstinence from dairy products and eggs as well as meat, was observed during lent. In their respective ways they are both symbols of new life and a fresh start.

Should you happen along the main road that passes through my village in front of the parish church at about midnight, while the Easter Vigil services are going on inside, you might see an even more singular appearance, a small rocket-like object wizzing over your head. It is the Easter dove, symbol of the sending of the Holy Spirit, made of paper mâché, with fire crackers for a tail.

The priest sets it off with the flame from the Paschal candle and it flies along a wire that runs from the sanctuary of the church, down the main aisle, out the door, across the street, where it is attached to a house on the other side of the road and, if all goes well, it traces its trajectory back in reverse to the altar. This is a replication in miniature of the same ritual performed on a grander scale on Easter morning in Florence between the Duomo and the baptistry of the cathedral. Even those who can usually be found playing cards in the café during liturgical ceremonies gather outside the village church to cheer the dove along its way. The first time I attended these services I was determined to maintain a duly detached and dignified composure but it was impossible not to be caught up in the fun and join in the spontaneous applause that accompanies the event.

On Easter day the dove alights on tables all over Italy in the form of a traditional sweet bread called *colomba pasquale*. This is a kind of porous sponge cake, usually with candied orange rind (peel) mixed in, sprinkled with crystallized sugar and studded with toasted almonds. Like the Christmas bread, *panettone*, from which it differs in form but not in substance, it originated in the far north of Italy and has been widely popularized by the large industrial bakeries who turn them out by the millions. My local baker makes a

A lustrous selection from over sixty
varieties of handmade chocolates
produced by Roberto Catinari.

somewhat smaller and superior version, richer and more dense, which I like lightly toasted with Easter morning coffee.

The Easter egg, however, is easily the most popular food item of the holiday. Italian children, showing a wisdom beyond their years, do not hunt the hard-boiled variety but demand really big chocolate ones that are hollow on the inside and contain a surprise, usually some sort of trinket whose value is relative to the price of the egg. Every season at my local café a garishly decorated monster egg that weighs in at about 10 pounds/5 kilos and stands at least 3.2 feet/1 metre high, worth many thousand lire, is sold in lottery at round 5000 lire a ticket. Since I have never won, or even bought a chance for that matter, I have no idea what surprise awaits the lucky winner, although I envision a scene from one of those American movies of the forties when they brought in the cake at a bachelor party.

Absolutely the most beautiful and delicious Easter eggs (with superior surprises) are made in the town of Agliana near Pistoia by Roberto Catinari, *cioccola-taio*, master artisan in chocolate. I tasted my first Catinari confection years ago at the restaurant of Badia a Coltibuono in Chianti, which was managed by Roberto's brother, Giannetto. It was in the form of a tiny flask of wine that was actually filled with Coltibuono's Classico.

Chocolates with other Tuscan liquid fillings, like Vin Santo and *grappa* and several fruit liquers as well, are a speciality of his shop. I once watched while bottles of one of the most prestigious and expensive Tuscan aquavits were being poured into hundreds of little moulds in the form of a grape bunch for an order the producer had commissioned. One soon learns to discern their various shapes from the ones with solid centres or runs the risk of dribbling the contents down the front of a freshly laundered shirt. The trick is to pop them into your mouth whole. Your taste-buds will be delighted with the effect.

Roberto Catinari grew up in a small town in the mountains of Pistoia where his parents owned a *pensione*. Like his sister before him and his brother after, and thousands of other young men and women from the poorer regions of Tuscany, he emigrated to Switzerland in search of employment, in the mid-Fifties when he was seventeen. First he worked as a dishwasher in restaurants and then he found a job washing pots and pans in a pastry and chocolate factory near Zurich. Twenty years later he was head of production. His employer had spotted not only a boy with an appetite for chocolate but a promising young man with an aptitude for this exacting craft.

In 1974, Roberto returned to Pistoia and, with his wife as assistant, began making chocolates using the kitchen of the family *pensione* as a workshop. He started with an initial investment that included some old moulds he had brought from Switzerland and a couple hundred kilos of chocolate paste. Eight years later, during which he had taken his product on the road throughout Tuscany and succeeded in building an appreciative and loyal clientele, he opened his own factory and shop in Agliana. Now he employs ten persons, several of whom are serving their three-year apprenticeship, and uses over fifteen tons of chocolate paste annually, which he buys in Italy, Belgium and Switzerland.

Downstairs in his shop Roberto displays an assortment of over sixty varieties of hand-made *cioccolatini*, dark, light and white with solid, cream and liquid centres, in the shape of truffles, walnuts, seashells, chestnuts and mushrooms. They are rich and smooth (he uses a minimum of fifty-two per cent cocoa) and lustrious, the sign, he tells me, of superior confections. His most requested chocolate is *gianduja*, a hazelnut cream that he also makes in large slabs with chopped nuts inside and studded with whole nuts on the outside. For connoisseurs and cooks, he makes blocks of smoky dark, bitter chocolate containing sixty-seven per cent cocoa. As you taste your way through a brightly coloured series of wafers you come across some unusual flavours, a dark chocolate with a tang of lemon, another with a refreshing hint of fennel and one that would have pleased the ancient Aztecs, a white chocolate wafer with a pinch of chilli powder.

His workshop is perhaps most famous for its sculptures. Roberto fashions chocolate into horse-shoes, tennis rackets, bicycles, wine bottles, keys and gardening tools. There is practically no shape he will not undertake upon special request. Recently he constructed a turreted castle that stands 3 feet/90cm.

Roberto Catinari, Master *Cioccolataio*, in the shop beneath his small factory in Agliana, near Pistoia.

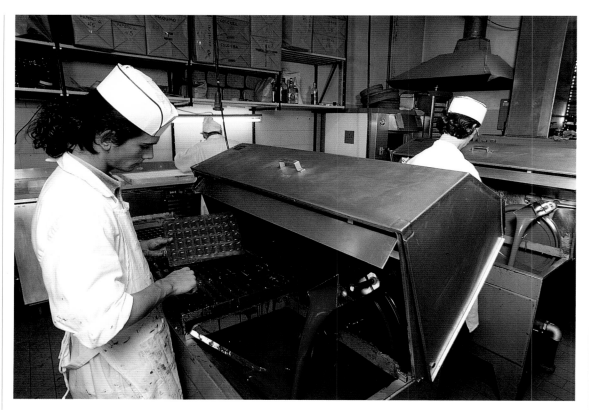

Two young apprentices working with dark and light chocolate perfect their skills in this exacting craft.

Although he steadfastly refuses a steady stream of requests to export his products, for fear he might be forced to industrialize, some of these sculptures have been sent to Germany and the United States.

Roberto calls Easter 'the feast of chocolate' and starts gearing his workshop for the event shortly after the Christmas holidays. He moulds chocolate into artistically decorated rabbits, chickens, ducks and an entire line of Disneyesque figures. An excited child might break open one of his gorgeous and luscious eggs and find a small camera or a cassette recorder with ear phones, and a mother might find a personalized piece of expensive jewellery. My favourite is an elegant *colomba pasquale*, Easter dove, whose feathers are a handsome combination of dark, light and white chocolates. The only problem is that it is really too beautiful to eat but somehow that scruple is shortly overcome. Lately Roberto has taken up oil painting as a hobby, an attempt, perhaps, to apply his artistic touch to a more enduring medium.

Tartufi Fondenti alla Catinari

CHOCOLATE TRUFFLES

This is Roberto Catinari's basic truffle recipe which he varies by adding coffee, Cognac, rum and other flavours to the mixture. Instead of rolling the balls in powdered chocolate he coats them in chocolate by dipping them in the mixture held at 79°F/27°C. It is not difficult to mould the mixture into a shape that at least vaguely resembles a little egg. Makes about 40 truffles.

4fl oz/125ml (½ cup) double (heavy) cream
8oz/250g bitter-sweet chocolate, cut in small pieces
2oz/60g (¾ cup) cocoa powder

Bring the cream to a boil in a copper or heavy-bottomed saucepan. As soon as it reaches the boil, start adding the chocolate, stirring constantly. When it has all been added, remove from heat and stir very well. Set aside to cool.

When the chocolate is slightly set, make individual balls by rolling a teaspoonful of the mixture in the palm of your hand. Roll the balls in the cocoa powder to coat lightly. Keep in the refrigerator but serve at room temperature.

While Tuscan *bambini* are spoiling their appetites with chocolate eggs, Tuscan mammas are busy preparing lamb for Easter Sunday dinner. They tell me that the authentic Tuscan way to cook this meat is *rifatto*, which means stewed. I imagine this originates from times when mutton rather than the luxury of milk-fed lamb was the family fare even for feastdays. The loin is cut into pieces (the leg is normally roasted), and simmered for a couple of hours in olive oil, garlic, rosemary, tomatoes and red wine. The slow cooking makes it tender and juicy. Anna, my neighbour, prepares *capretto*, kid, for her family's Easter dinner in the same way. The difference, she says, is that this meat is more tender and delicately flavoured than lamb and, as the main course for the Easter meal, she claims it represents an even older tradition in these parts.

For years my Easter lamb was prepared by Romola Chini, the family cook at Badia a Coltibuono vineyard. She roasts it the Tuscan way, very, very slowly for at least two hours until the outside becomes crusty and the flesh so tender it practically falls from the bone. A pinkish, transalpine *gigot*, in the French style, would strike her as a bit barbarian. When the joint is ready, she cuts it into succulent chunks rather than carving it into slices, and serves it on a platter surrounded with fresh spring spinach sautéed in olive oil.

I have a personal preference for preparing my favourite meat. Every year around Easter time a Sardinian friend brings me a specially selected lamb from his flock. He lives in the Mugello, an area in north-eastern Tuscany at the foot of the Appenines. When you drive down the Italian penisola from the cattle-raising regions of northern Italy, the Mugello is the first place where you see sheep grazing. They become more numerous the further south you go.

The lamb will only be about forty days old. Any younger it would still have too much of its baby fat. A couple of weeks older it would have started to eat grass and have lost some of its milk-fed tenderness. Alive it weighed about 6 pounds/12 kilos. Prepared for the fires it only weighs about 4 pounds/8 kilos but plenty to feed a dozen hungry friends.

We roast it whole in a big, old, brick, outdoor bread oven that my neighbours reactivated for the feast. Inside there is plenty of space to place roasting pans full of endives, onions and potatoes next to the lamb marinated in garlic, thyme, oregano, olive oil and white wine. Mastering the method of cooking with *caldo bianco*, white heat, involves a fair amount of trial and error and it is inevitably quite late before we all sit down to dinner but the entire process stimulates both thirst and appetite and the end result is immensely gratifying.

Agnello Arrosto alla Romola
ROMOLA'S ROAST LAMB

Romola Chini, the family cook at Badia a Coltibuono winery, always starts her roasts — lamb, pork and chicken but not roast beef — in an unheated oven and cooks them slowly for a long time so all the fat has time to dissolve, leaving the outer part crisp and the inside tender and loose on the bone.

Serves 6.
2½lb/1.25kg baby lamb, leg and loin
3 cloves garlic
3 fresh sprigs rosemary, roughly chopped
Salt and pepper
4fl oz/125ml (½ cup) extra-virgin olive oil
Spinach sautéed in olive oil to serve

Rinse the lamb and pat dry. Divide into portions and chine the bone.

With a pestle and mortar, crush the garlic, add the rosemary, salt and pepper and blend with a fork. Insert a little of this mixture between the portions of meat and add more salt and pepper.

Place the lamb in a roasting pan and pour over the olive oil. Put into an unheated oven and set at 350°F/180°C/Gas mark 4. Cook for at least 2 hours. When ready to serve, separate the portions, arrange on a warm platter, surround with the spinach and serve.

Spinaci Saltati
SPINACH SAUTÉED IN OLIVE OIL

In Romola's family, spinach is the traditional vegetable served with spring lamb. She finds its fresh, grassy taste a perfect balance to the sweetness of the meat. For sautéeing the spinach, Romola uses some of the oil from the cooking juices of the lamb. *Saltati* means 'jumped' and refers to the method of sautéeing the spinach very quickly, making the leaves jump in the pan, which professionals literally do with a flick of the wrist.

Serves 6.
1lb/3½oz/600g fresh spinach leaves
60ml/2fl oz (¼ cup) extra-virgin olive oil
1 clove garlic, roughly chopped
salt and pepper

Rinse the spinach well in several changes of water, then cook for about 5 minutes with just the water that clings to the leaves, until tender. Drain and squeeze dry.

Sauté the garlic with the oil in a large frying pan (skillet) until slightly coloured.

Add the spinach, salt and pepper and sauté for a couple of minutes, turning the spinach leaves over several times. Serve on the platter surrounding the lamb.

Moulds in the form of a grape bunch,
pressed in flour, are filled with *grappa*
mixed with liquified sugar. After the
sugar has crystallized and formed a
thin shell, they will be coated with
dark chocolate.

A NOMADIC BEEKEEPER & MONOFLORAL TREE HONEYS

Antonio Prato is as industrious, or almost, as the bees he keeps. He has also, perhaps through long association, developed a few of their physical characteristics, large intense eyes set under a broad forehead and thick eyebrows. In late spring he even has a buzz about him that reaches a high pitch as his production period nears its peak.

Antonio is what is known in his profession as a nomadic beekeeper, specializing in mountain mono-floral tree honeys. In his white Fiat pick-up loaded with forty or so brightly painted hives he follows the flowering season around the woods and forests of Tuscany. It is a back-breaking job. He must carry his hives well off the main road to where, at that moment, a single type of flower is in highest concentration. The hours are hectic as well. Bees are best transported during the cool hours after sunset and the hives must be in place before sunrise, in time for the foraging bees to scout the new territory and bring back samples of pollen to the other workers so they can set out.

Almost twenty years ago, while studying political science in Florence, Antonio began working with bees as a hobby. When his interest quickly developed into a passion, he changed his field to agriculture, specializing in apiculture. He now operates his own bee and honey business, tending over 300 hives and their some fifteen million occupants who, in an average year, make about twelve tons of honey.

Early on Antonio discovered that the wooded hills and mountains of Tuscany provided the most congenial working environment both for him and his bees. It is relatively uncontaminated compared to the cultivated fields where insecticides have made life hazardous for bees as well as other living things. The complex eco-system is also more interesting and he enjoys the company of the other animals, curious deer, cautious wild boar and the pheasants that insist on building their nests between his hives.

The bees he breeds are, of course, pure Italian, the *apis ligustica*, 'best bee in the world', Antonio says. I am one easily convinced that anything Italian having to do with food is the best but it was news even to me that Italy produces a superior race of bees. And like other fine products made in Italy, the *ligustica* has been exported to other countries, especially to England and the United States.

It is small and slender with a dark brown hairy chest and yellow and brown bands on its body. Antonio often comments on the similarity between bees and human beings. His theory seems to hold true here. He tells me that the Italian *ligustica* is mild mannered and does not have the 'bad habit' of stinging easily but only under stress. It has a strong disposition to breed rearing and is a big eater, particularly shrewd at finding sources of pollen and nectar. Not surprisingly, given their national origin, they are also talented architects and skilful engineers. No other bees, Antonio claims, construct such beautiful honey comb as the Italian.

The *ligustica* possesses two physical characteristics that are of particular importance when you work with Antonio. Their small and slender build make them aerodynamically ideal for flying around the steep inclines and limited open spaces of the wooded hills and mountains of Tuscany. Most importantly of all, they are endowed with an exceptionally long tongue. This is an invaluable attribute for collecting nectar from tree blossoms which tend to be more protected on the branch than field flowers.

Variations of colour and texture of the
monofloral mountain tree honeys
produced by Antonio Prato.

By mid-March Antonio's bees are already out and about, buzzing around the flowering fields of wild and cultivated rape, gathering nectar from the lemon-yellow flowers and converting it into honey for themselves. They go to work for Antonio shortly afterwards when tree heather, *erica arborea*, comes into bloom. This tall-growing Mediterranean variety of heather produces an ash-white, slightly fragrant bell-shaped flower that is high in nectar. It grows in profusion in the neighbouring hills of Chianti so Antonio does not have to take his bees very far for their first commercial job of the season. Tree heather flowers for almost four weeks but during what is normally a rainy period, so unfortunately the bees are often forced to stay inside. In this case, Antonio

In early Spring tree heather flowers in nectar rich blossoms.

usually spends his time baby-sitting new broods which will be ready to go to work in a couple of months, just in time to help bring in the end-of-the-season crop. When the weather is clement and his bees are able to gather nectar from the heather, they prepare a honey that has an intensely floral aroma, is reddish amber in colour and pleasantly sweet.

Towards the end of the second week of May, Antonio moves his bees about 30 miles/18 kilometres up the valley of the Arno river, where *acacia robinia* trees, sometimes called false acacia, are in full bloom. From its cream-white, pea-like flowers that hang in pendulous bunches, the bees will gather almost half of Antonio's annual production. Because this straw-yellow acacia honey remains fluid (most unprocessed honeys crystallize) and is delicately flavoured, it is one of the most suitable for use in the kitchen. Before the invention of refined sugar, honey was the most frequently used sweetener in cooking. Many Tuscan sweets, Sienese *panforte* and *ricciarelli* biscuits (cookies) in particular, are still made with acacia honey instead of sugar.

As the weather warms Antonio prepares his hives for the longest trek of the season. He sets out with his bees for the chestnut forests that grow in the high mountain regions of the Pratomagno in the Apennines and the Garfagnano in the province of Lucca, about 150 miles/90 kilometres away. These lovely and generous sweet chestnut trees, *castanea sativa*, produce tiny, stemless flowers sheltered within pale, greenish-yellow catkins, which will be followed by spiny burrs containing an autumnal harvest of red-brown nuts. With their long tongue the *ligustica* extracts a delicious nectar from these flowers that they transform into my favourite honey. It has a beautiful

Antonio Prato uncapping frames of comb before extracting the honey.

deep amber colour, a nutty aroma and rich flavour with an appealingly bitter aftertaste.

If the weather co-operates, the bees can work for practically a full month in these forests, well into summer. Antonio first sets his hives at the lower elevations, 2275 feet/700 metres, and gradually moves them up to 2600 feet/800 metres, where the chestnuts are replaced by forests of oak and silver fir. A curious phenomenon takes place when the temperature is hot and humid. The trees and certain aphids and insects feeding on their sap excrete a sweet liquid. This 'honeydew' is gathered and stored by the bees. The result is a thick, dark honey called *manna*. (When honeydew is left on the plant, it granulates rapidly and biblical scholars think that this substance might be what 'fell from heaven' and nourished the Israelites during the exodus from Egypt.) Exegesis apart, Christie, Antonio's American wife, tells me that *manna* is a good substitute for maple syrup on Sunday morning pancakes eaten in exile abroad.

The Italian bee constructs particularly beautiful honeycomb.

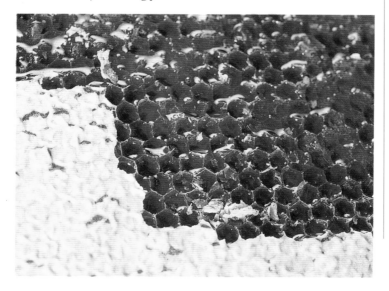

By mid-summer, when their sources of nectar have dried up, the honey bees spend most of their time trying to keep the queen cool and comfortable in the hive, while Antonio is kept busy processing their honey. During this period and on into early autumn, he can usually be found working in his honeyhouse, a small, ancient barn that he converted into a work-shop, where the air is sweet with the pungent aroma of raw honey.

Since Antonio neither homogenizes nor pasteur-izes his honey, which would destroy not only much of its flavour but some of its nutritive value, his task requires a minimum of equipment and a maximum of manual labour. He must first uncap hundreds of frames of honeycomb by scraping away with a wide fork the wax the bees have used to seal in the honey. He then extracts it by means of a simple centrifuge machine which spins it out of the comb. In a few minutes the rich, thick liquid begins to run out the bottom into stainless steel containers. Before bottling he strains the honey twice, first through a wire then a cloth mesh. Because he does not treat his bees with antibiotics but keeps them healthy by constant care and cleaning of the hives, their wax is much in demand by producers of cosmetics.

During the mild days of early autumn Antonio's bees conclude their production cycle with a honey made from nectar gathered from late blooming mountain flora that he labels *mille fiori*, a thousand flowers. In November and December Antonio assumes the role of carpenter, repairing old hives and building new ones. Then, once he has settled his bees in for the winter, he finally has time to enjoy a holiday that will certainly include some Christmas sweets containing his own honey.

Spaghetti alla Ricotta e Miele

— SPAGHETTI WITH RICOTTA AND HONEY SAUCE —

This is a recipe Antonio remembers from his youth. He suggests using chestnut honey. Its slightly bitter aftertaste together with the oregano gives the sauce a savoury flavour.

Serves 6.
salt
1lb/500g spaghetti
1lb/500g fresh ricotta cheese
1tbsp/15ml chestnut honey
1tsp/5ml dried oregano

Bring a large saucepan of salted water to the boil. Add the spaghetti and cook until *al dente*, or just tender.

While the spaghetti is cooking, transfer the ricotta to a warm serving bowl and, whisking lightly, gradually add enough water from the spaghetti pot to bring the ricotta to the consistency of a sauce. Whisk in the honey and oregano and add salt to taste. Drain the pasta and transfer to the serving bowl. Toss well and serve at once.

Gelato al Miele di Castagno

— CHESTNUT BLOSSOM HONEY ICE CREAM —

Antonio Prato also keeps the bees and makes the honey for the Badia a Coltibuono vineyard in Chianti. Many years ago I brought a jar of this estate's chestnut blossom honey to Alice Waters, the proprietor of Chez Panisse, the celebrated restaurant in Berkeley, California. She gave it to her chef, Paul Bertolli, who used it to make this ice cream. The recipe is taken from their book, *Chez Panisse Cooking.*

As a quick alternative for obtaining the same inimitable flavour, heat the honey in a pan, and while it is still hot, drizzle it over rich vanilla ice cream.

6tbsp/90ml chestnut honey
2tsbp/30ml clover honey
8fl oz/250ml (1 cup) single (light) cream
1¾oz/50g (¼ cup) sugar
16fl oz/500ml (2 cups) double (heavy) cream
6 large egg yolks

Warm the chestnut and clover honeys in a small saucepan. In another saucepan, heat the single (light), sugar, and half of the double (heavy) cream and stir until the sugar is dissolved.

Whisk the egg yolks in a bowl. Add the cream mixture to the yolks, whisking constantly together. Return the mixture to the saucepan and cook over low heat, stirring constantly, until the custard is thick and coats the spoon. Strain through a fine sieve (strainer) into the remaining 8fl oz/250ml (1 cup) double (heavy) cream. Stir in the warmed honeys.

Chill and freeze in an ice-cream maker. Serve slightly soft in chilled bowls.

Right: Two goblets of creamy chestnut blossom honey ice cream.

FLORENTINE FOOD

If you have the luxury of choice, the best time to visit Florence, 'the most visited city in Europe,' is the month of May. A lull occurs between the invading hordes who descend from the north at Easter and the arrival of summer travellers from over the seas. Temperatures are mild and conducive to expending the energy that being a diligent tourist, even on your own territory, demands.

When I go into the Big City the pleasures I most enjoy, gastronomically at least, are bustling food markets, gourmet stores, elegant cafés, lively *trattorie* and restaurants where you feel you are eating out, instead of in, all of which are difficult to find in the provinces.

Luckily for me, who, like most country folk, wearies quickly of city commotion, a little island exists in the centre of Florence where you need venture no further than a few yards in any direction to enjoy the best of all of these. Except for a market already in place, this eater's paradise is the creation of a young Florentine couple, Benedetta Vitali and Fabio Picchi. In 1979, they began their celebrated Cibrèo restaurant and a tiny *trattoria* behind the kitchen. In 1985, they opened a fine food shop next door and in 1989, a small café across the street. A new date was added recently, when in 1990, Cibrèo opened in Tokyo.

Cibrèo has the great good fortune to have one of Florence's two main food markets in its backyard. *Il Mercato di Sant'Ambrogio* is smaller than the immense and amazing *Mercato Centrale* on the other side of town but it has a unique attraction. At the outdoor stalls surrounding the market building you find some of the city's finest produce. One section is reserved for the farmers from nearby Rosano, whose carts are heaped with piles of home-grown vegetables, wild salad greens and herbs.

In the chilly, early morning hours when the venders warm themselves around bonfires that they feed with wooden slats from discarded crates, the tall, robust Rubenesque figure of Fabio, clad in chief's garb, can be seen striding down the lanes of stands, chatting and joking with his suppliers. He reminds a young woman to ask her husband to deliver a promised crate of fresh broad (fava) beans that he intends to use in a salad with slices of *pecorino* cheese. Fabio tells me they are recent arrivals at the market but because their produce is so outstanding he immediately began buying from them. Now he feels a chill coming from the direction of the nearby stall of his 'ex' supplier. As general policy he trades with two or three producers to keep prices competitive and quality high.

Fabio purchases his fish from the *pescheria Silvestri*, directly across the street from the restaurant. Here there are no frozen halibut from Greenland, nor grouper from New Zealand, only a limited choice and supply of fresh fish from native waters. Today he selects salmon trout that he will bake in foil and a bag of mussels to marinate in olive oil and lemon with tender spring artichokes.

First thing in the morning, before leaving home, Fabio buys most of his meat from his village butcher but now he stops at a little cart parked in the street on the corner to pick up a Florentine speciality at the tripe stand of Signora Maria Masti. The Signora's husband works for the consortium of tripe processors so she is assured of choice quality.

Tripe, *trippa* in Italian, is the lining of the stomach of animals who chew their cud. There are several

The cupola and polychrome
campanile of Florence's Duomo define
the skyline of Tuscany's capital.

Above: Husband and wife team, Fabio Picchi and Benedetta Vitali, creators of Cibrèo. *Right:* Small, violet coloured globe artichokes in Florence's central market.

and marinates it in olive oil and vinegar with a little very finely chopped onion, celery, carrot, garlic and parsley. A small bowl of it is always brought to the table along with several other *antipasti*. It is truly delicious, although it is better to encourage companions to taste before you tell them what it is.

Tripe vendors, more precisely tripe carters, known as *trippai ambulanti*, represent a venerable Florentine tradition. Until well after World War II, there were some forty of them scattered throughout the city. Now their number is down to less than a dozen but these seem to do a brisk business, especially selling tripe *panini*, crunchy rolls stuffed with *trippa*. In the morning and again in the early evening, *trippai* station their carts and umbrellas, and in several cases vans, at strategic spots in the old inner city neighbourhoods and at the entrance gates to the city. Each cart or van is fitted with stainless steel pots where the tripe is boiled and a counter on which it is cut to order.

When Fabio craves a mid-morning snack, he heads down the block to *Piazza dei Ciompi* for a tripe sandwich. (Signora Maria only deals in the pure product.) There, literally in a little hole-in-the-wall on

kinds of tripe, according to the different compartments of a ruminant's stomach. The most common is descriptively called *cuffia*, meaning bonnet or bathing cap. San Bernardino the popular fourteenth-century Tuscan preacher, chastised the women of Florence for their vanity, wearing frilly caps that looked, he said, like pieces of tripe.

Florentines buy tripe from their local vendor already cleaned and partially cooked and then take it home to prepare *trippa alla fiorentina*. They cut it into strips, simmer it in a highly seasoned tomato sauce and serve it *al dente*, like pasta, with lots of freshly grated Parmesan cheese. Every day Fabio buys a large bag of tripe that Signora Maria has sliced for him

the corner, a young Florentine named Marco carries on the old tradition at one of the most characteristic locations in the city. Fabio orders a *panino* with *lampredotto*, considered by connoisseurs the tastiest bit of tripe. Following the traditional rubric, before serving the sandwich, Marco sticks a fork into the top half of the roll and dips it into the pot of warm broth, just enough to moisten the rim.

I must admit that I prefer to buy my snack a few doors down at Panetteria Ciompi, one of the two bakeries that supplies bread to Cibrèo. A steady stream of customers flows in and out of the crowded shop, carrying away large rounds of Tuscan saltless white bread and darker loaves made with whole wheat. *Schiacciate*, thin, chewy flatbreads with various savoury seasonings, are a speciality, as are a few sweet seasonal breads, like *pan di ramerino*, buns with rosemary and raisins. Judging from all the munchings going on in the street, these rarely make it all the way home.

By 9 am, marketing done and a dozen other details seen to, Fabio is in the kitchen, where his young assistant chef, Patrick, and four cooks have been at work for over an hour preparing for the day's cooking, peeling potatoes and piles of garlic, cleaning capers, chopping onions, carrots, celery and parsley for the *battuto* that is the foundation for many of Cibrèo's dishes, filleting fish and deboning rabbits.

They use the white-tiled *trattoria*, a small room behind the even smaller kitchen, as additional work space. Originally it was a *vineria*, a shop that sold flask wine by the glass to the market crowd. Now it seats some twenty diners at shared tables and serves a limited version of the restaurant menu. When it is being used as a workroom by the cooks, the tables and chairs are pushed to one side and reassembled again in time for lunch.

Meanwhile, ten pots are simmering on the huge wood-burning stove that takes up a good third of the tiny kitchen, and by 9:15 Fabio starts to cook. Besides taste and talent, teamwork and timing seem to be the secrets to the success of the Cibrèo kitchen. The restricted space has imposed the kind of discipline and control that encourages rather than limits creativity.

While Fabio is concocting some of the soups that have become a Cibrèo hallmark – on today's menu there is a *passata* of sweet yellow peppers, a white cabbage, bean and bread *ribollita* and a fish *zuppa* – Patrick concentrates on several specialities that require single-minded attention. He wraps lamb brains with butter, lemon and nutmeg in foil, and stuffs pigeon with a pear filling.

Laura, whom Fabio is training to take his place when he is away and the only woman in the kitchen,

Right: Strips of marinated tripe and little rounds of goat cheese are among the *antipasti* served at Cibrèo.

attends to today's moulds, tuna, Swiss chard and cheese. Using a pastry bag, Maurizio fills chicken necks with a mixture of minced (ground) beef, Parmesan cheese, grated lemon rind (peel) and breadcrumbs soaked in milk. Adamo is perfecting just one dish, *involtini*, meat rolls containing mortadella, artichokes, olives and parsley, that Patrick will fry afterwards in butter with a splash of wine. Eric, the most recent arrival, is still peeling and chopping away in the workroom.

Everything progresses remarkably smoothly as dishes go on and off the stove and in and out of the ovens. You sense that Fabio is confident and content with his young team. He calls for ingredients, gives timing instructions for the six veal tails and one pig's trotter that are cooking for the evening meal, greets the girl that has come to arrange flowers, amicably argues politics with the man who delivers wood, and absorbs a couple of crises (two waiters are blocked in traffic due to a protest march and will be late getting in to set tables, and a VIP wants a reservation but the restaurant is fully booked).

At 12:30 sharp, Fabio, Patrick and the two head waiters hold their daily tasting critique: the bread soup is a little too thick, Laura's meatloaf is superb, the chicken necks are slightly under seasoned, the *polenta* is particularly good. Some minor adjustments are made and at 12:50 they are ready to serve.

All this while, across the street in the kitchen of the café, Benedetta, Fabio's wife, has been busy baking desserts. When she and Fabio began the restaurant fifteen years ago they both did the marketing and cooking and took turns serving their customers. Now Benedetta has the leisure, so to speak, to specialize doing what she enjoys best, making two hundred and fifty portions of dessert for the restaurant and café. My favourite is her richly satisfying *pastiera di grano*, a sweet pastry crust spread with a mixture of ricotta, whole-wheat grain and sugar flavoured with vanilla and orange-flower water.

Benedetta's assistant also sees to the café's select menu. Service begins with a continental breakfast and continues until two in the morning with coffee and drinks. Cibrèo Caffé is one of these rare and welcome places in Italy where you can lunch lightly, elegantly and comfortably, enjoying such delicacies as a plate of *prosciutto di Sauris* from Friuli, perhaps combining it with a dish of *bocconcini*, little 'mouth fulls' of fresh buffalo's milk mozzarella from Battipaglia, or a warm bowl of *passatelli in brodo*, a rich chicken broth brought over from the restaurant with little noodles of Parmesan cheese and breadcrumbs added.

The café itself is a little gem. Too little for total comfort perhaps but still a gem. I remember the evening a few years ago when Fabio invited me to come take a look at his 'new café'. What he proudly showed me was a gutted room with two splendid eighteenth-century carved wooden entrance doors that he had just hung. First things first. He already had a piece of antique parquet flooring that was looking for a home. Soon afterwards a friend came up with a superb turn-of-the-century, wood-and-glass panelled wall from an old pastry shop, and for the bar, an ornate wood counter that was originally in a pharmacy. The *coup de grâce*, which almost literally fell from heaven, is a painted renaissance ceiling which came from a monastery in the Florentine countryside.

One gets the impression that what Benedetta and Fabio really had in mind when they decided to open their café was to provide a convenient and congenial

My favourite seat in Florence, at
Cibrèo Caffé, in a corner next to the
antique cherry panelled wall and
old oak bar.

place where they could relax after working in the restaurant. In fact, at about three every afternoon they can be found there huddled at a corner table, having a bite to eat and discussing transportation logistics for their four school-aged children. Then Benedetta goes back to her baking and Fabio heads home where he cooks an early supper for the family before returning to the restaurant for the evening.

It is time for me to walk across the street to the Cibrèo fine-food shop and pick up a few things to take back to the country. The store is full of delicious and interesting items, some expensive, some less so, all the very best of their kind. Many are regional specialities, normally impossible to find outside their place of origin. There are fruit jams from northern Italy; Sicilian orange marmalade; *babà napoletani*, small golden pastries soaked in rum syrup; anchovy fillets preserved in truffle-flavoured olive oil; *follarelli*, little packets of juicy, partially dried sweet white grapes with a sprinkle of candied citrus rind (peel) and hand wrapped in chestnut leaves; pasta from Puglia and *arborio* rice from Verona: and, at Christmas, *panettone* from Bini in Milano that weighs 2 pounds/4 kilos and comes in a container that looks

like a hat box. For the Florentines, there are tins of English teas and biscuits (cookies), Russian caviar and French wines.

The word *'cibrèo'* originally referred to a delicious Renaissance dish, still made today, consisting of chicken giblets and combs, sautéed in butter and onion with egg yolks and lemon added. It was used as a stuffing in other dishes but was so good it was also eaten on its own. Caterina de'Medici was said to be inordinately fond of it. It subsequently acquired the secondary meaning of an abundance of good things. With their Cibrèo Fabio and Benedetta have given it yet a third.

Grocery shopping can work up an appetite and should you feel like a little something before setting off home, there is a sweet surprise in store hidden just a block or so behind the market at No. 8 on the busy *Piazza Beccaria*. It is called Dolci & Dolcezze, 'Sweets & Sweet Things'. The shop, even from the outside, painted mint green like the icing of a *cassata siciliana*, with two delicious display windows, looks good enough to eat.

Inside is irresistible. Owner and pastry chef, Giulio Corti, is a man with a refined aesthetic sense for both decor and desserts. His taste in interior decoration is baroque. A large painting hanging behind the counter appears to be a seventeenth-century still life in the Italian style, depicting flowers and fruits and sweet foods, until you notice that they are reproductions of the same confections on the shelves of the shop. His cakes, on the other hand, are composed with a simplicity and purity of colour and form that is almost oriental.

Giulio is a master artisan who found his true vocation only after having studied law and worked as

Reflected in the mirror of a souvenir shop across its great piazza, the façade of the church of Santa Croce, whose interior is the most richly adorned in all of Florence.

Elegant interior of Giulio Corti's Dolci & Dolcezze, Sweets & Sweet Things.

a portrait photographer for several years. In a way, he heeded the call of his taste-buds for the kind of sweets he had adored as a child but now found himself discarding after the first bite. Something, he decided, had gone wrong and he was determined to try and set it right. With cookery books in hand and his wife at his side, he started baking for friends and a few fine restaurants (Cibrèo among them) in a little shop on the outskirts of Florence. He succeeded and in 1990, opened his shop in *Piazza Beccaria*.

Of course, what had changed for the worse, he discovered, were the quality of ingredients and the process of production. Today, Giulio tells me, you could produce pastry merely by assembling pre-fabricated components parts from a can. Instead, he and his five assistants start early ('but not too early') in the morning with fresh eggs, butter, flour and sugar, rolling out *pasta frolla*, sweet pastry dough, by hand. What has not been sold by closing time goes to a home for the elderly. The *dolci* are tarts of dense, dark chocolate and seasonal fruits, as well as moulds of beautiful bavarian cream flavoured with mint, hazelnut and coffee. The *dolcezze* are cookies, jars of creamy chocolate spreads and fresh fruit marmalades.

Dolci & Dolcezze also provides an international selection of fine dessert wines and they will pour you a glass to enjoy with one or two of their tiny tarts. At this point you might consider catching a movie at the neighbouring cinema. Then you can stay on for an early supper at Cibrèo.

Spring Luncheon Menu at Cibrèo

SFORMATI DI FAGIOLINI VERDI E TONNO

Tuna and bean moulds

MINESTRONE CON BASILICO E PINOLI

Vegetable soup with basil and pine nuts

CONIGLIO RIPIENO ARROSTO

Roast stuffed rabbit

CARCIOFI AL TEGAME

Sautéed artichokes

CROSTATA DI PERE

Pear pie

The little tuna and bean moulds are colourful, elegant and delicious. At Cibrèo, just one is served at a table for four together with a selection of several other antipasti. The recipe could be adapted to fill a large ring mould and served as the main course for a light, warm-weather luncheon. The soup is Fabio Picchi's Tuscan variation of a Genoese minestrone. The only complicated part about the stuffed roast rabbit is deboning it, which you might try to convince your butcher to do. Benedetta's pear pie is superb.

Sformati di Fagiolini Verdi e Tonno
TUNA AND BEAN MOULDS

Serves 6.
100oz/300g young green beans, topped and tailed
100oz/300g canned tuna fish, well drained
2 oz/60 g (½ cup) unsalted butter
1 clove garlic
2 tbsp/30 ml extra-virgin olive oil, plus a little extra for serving
pinch dried oregano
pinch dried marjoram
1 tsp/5 ml finely chopped fresh parsley
salt and pepper

Tuna and green bean mould dressed with olive oil.

One of Cibrèo's satisfying soups: creamed spinach enriched with dollops of olive oil, ricotta, croutons, grated Parmesan cheese and chopped chicken liver.

Boil the beans in lightly salted water until just tender. Drain. Line the bottom and sides of 6 ramekins or custard cups with slightly overlapping green beans.

Combine the remaining ingredients in a blender or food processor and process until smooth and soft, or combine them in a bowl and mash with a fork.

Fill the ramekins with the mixture and refrigerate for at least 1 hour. Carefully turn the ramekins out on to small plates and dress the moulds with olive oil.

Minestrone con Basilico e Pinoli
—— VEGETABLE SOUP WITH BASIL AND PINE NUTS ——

Serves 6.
1 large red onion
3 carrots, peeled
3 celery stalks
14 fl oz/400 m (1¾ cups) extra-virgin olive oil
salt
¼ head Savoy cabbage, shredded
5 courgettes (zucchini), dried
5 potatoes, peeled and diced
1 leek, sliced and well rinsed
1 spring onion (scallion), sliced
100 oz/300 g (1½ cups) cannellini beans, cooked
5 small bunches fresh basil
2 cloves garlic
5oz/150 g (scant 1 cup) pine nuts
3½ oz/100 g (7 tbsp) unsalted butter, softened
8 oz/250 g Parmesan cheese, finely grated

Chop together, as finely as possible, the onion, 1 carrot and 1 celery stalk and set aside.

In a large, deep pan, combine 5 fl oz/150 ml (⅔ cup) olive oil with the finely chopped vegetables and, stirring occasionally, fry gently over low heat until golden. Add the remaining vegetables and enough water to barely cover. Season with salt. Bring to the boil over medium heat and boil briskly for about 20 minutes or until the carrots, which take the longest time to cook, are tender. Add the beans and heat thoroughly.

Meanwhile, prepare the pesto. Combine the basil leaves, garlic, pine nuts, butter and 5 fl oz/150 ml (⅔ cup) olive oil in a blender or food processor, and blend until the basil and garlic are puréed. Add 5 oz/150 g Parmesan cheese and process until the sauce is smooth.

When the vegetables are cooked, remove the soup from the heat and stir in the pesto. Transfer the soup to a warm tureen and serve with the remaining olive oil and Parmesan cheese.

Coniglio Ripieno Arrosto
—— ROAST STUFFED RABBIT ——

Serves 6.
1 rabbit, boned
salt and pepper
3 slices *prosciutto*
3 slices crustless white bread
8 fl oz/250 ml (1 cup) milk
10 oz/300 g lean minced (ground) beef
3 oz/90 g Parmesan cheese, finely grated
4 eggs
pinch grated nutmeg
5 spring onions (scallions), green tops removed
1 tbsp/15 ml finely chopped fresh parsley
3½ fl oz/100 ml (7 tbsp) extra-virgin olive oil
8 fl oz/250 ml (1 cup) red wine

Vespe, motorized 'wasps', swarm on
the streets of Florence.

Spread the rabbit out flat on a board. Sprinkle lightly with salt and cover with the sliced *prosciutto*.

Soak the bread in the milk. Squeeze out the excess liquid and combine with the beef, Parmesan cheese, 1 egg, a little salt and pinch of nutmeg and pepper. Stir until thoroughly blended.

Blanch the spring onions (scallions) in boiling water for 3 minutes. Drain and set aside.

Whisk the 3 remaining eggs with the parsley and a pinch of salt. Make a flat, soft omelette in a large frying pan (skillet).

Roll the stuffing into a sausage shape about 2 in/5 cm wide and the length of the rabbit. Place it in the centre of the rabbit, adjusting the shape if necessary. Cut the omelette into strips about 3 in/7.5 cm wide and as long as possible. Arrange them over the stuffing. Cover the omelette with a layer of the spring onion (scallion) tops.

Wrap one side of the rabbit over the stuffing and cover it with the other side, then pin together with wooden toothpicks. The rolled rabbit should be (5-6 in/12.5-15 cm) wide. Tie well with string and remove the toothpicks. Place the rabbit in a roasting pan. Season lightly with salt and pour over the oil. Bake in a preheated 100°F/200°C/Gas mark 6 oven for 60 minutes, turning occasionally to brown well on all sides and gradually adding the wine so the cooking juices turn into a fairly thick sauce to serve with the sliced rabbit.

Carciofi al Tegame
SAUTÉED ARTICHOKES

Serves 6.
10 small globe artichokes
juice of 1 lemon
2 slices unsmoked bacon (slab bacon), ¼ in/5 cm thick, diced
2 cloves garlic, chopped
2 tbsp/30 ml finely chopped fresh parsley
5 fl oz/150 ml (⅔ cup) extra-virgin olive oil
salt and pepper
4 fl oz/125 ml (½ cup) stock or water

Prepare the artichokes by removing the tough outer leaves, central chokes and prickly spikes. Cut into quarters and immediately drop them into a bowl of water and lemon juice to prevent discoloration.

Combine the drained artichokes, bacon, garlic, parsley, oil, salt and plenty of pepper in a large, heavy-based frying pan (skillet). Add stock or water and stir well. Cover the pan and cook over medium heat for 10 to 15 minutes. After 10 minutes prick the stalks to test if they are ready, be careful not to overcook as artichokes tend to continue cooking after they have been removed from the heat. Serve piping hot.

Slices of roast stuffed rabbit decorated with sprigs of rosemary blossom.

Crostata di Pere

PEAR PIE

Serves 6.

PASTRY:
8 oz/250 g (2 sticks) unsalted butter, in small pieces
3½ oz/100 g (½ cup) granulated sugar
14 oz/400 g (3½ cups) plain (all-purpose) flour
1 egg yolk plus 1 whole egg
1 tbsp/15 ml milk to glaze

FILLING:
3 cooking pears, peeled, cored and diced
2 fl oz/60 ml (1¼ cup) tawny Port
2 tbsp/30 ml granulated sugar
1 oz/30 g seedless raisins
1 oz/30 g walnuts halved, coarsely chopped
1 oz/30 g pine nuts
pinch ground cinnamon

Tempting tarts in the window display of Dolci & Dolcezze.

To make the pastry, combine the butter, sugar, flour and egg yolk, as quickly as possible without handling it more than necessary or it will be tough. Wrap it in cling film (plastic wrap) and leave it to rest, chilled, for at least 2 hours.

Meanwhile, leave the pears to soak in the Port and sugar for at least 1 hour. Soak the raisins in lukewarm water for at least 20 minutes. Rinse, drain and set aside.

Combine all the ingredients for the filling and sprinkle them with the cinnamon.

Divide the pastry in half and line a 10 in/25 cm loose-bottomed pie pan with a thin layer of pastry. Roll the remaining pastry into a round the size of the pan. Fill the lined pan with the filling, including the Port and pear juice. Roll the second layer of pastry around a rolling pin and carefully unroll it to cover the pan. Press the edges of the top and bottom crusts together. Prick the top with fork in several places so the steam can escape during baking.

Brush the surface with the remaining whole egg and milk mixed together and transfer the pan to a pre-heated 400°F/200°C/gas mark 6 oven. Bake for about 40 minutes. Cool on a wire rack.

SUMMER

If you were to work it out right, you could eat at an outdoor *festa* in Tuscany practically everyday from mid-June to mid-September. These *feste* get underway with May Day celebrations and are in full swing by July. They provide the Tuscan with an occasion to indulge his appetite for eating, drinking and socializing in a congenial (and cool) atmosphere.

VILLA COOKING CLASSES & A BARONIAL BANQUET

It is not everyday that I am invited to dine in the castles of Chianti. The fact is, it only happens about ten times a year in early summer and autumn, when I tag along as hired help with the groups from Lorenza de'Medici's week-long cooking classes at Badia a Coltibuono. But since I have been doing it for the past ten years I must admit that I am beginning to feel right at home eating in baronial halls hung with Goblein tapestries and in Renaissance rooms with frescoed ceilings, served by waiters wearing livery and white gloves.

These grand meals conclude days that begin with a three-hour cooking class conducted by Lorenza in her family kitchen at Coltibuono. I show up when the students are ready to go to table, just in time to test the results of the morning's session in the kitchen. Although I have never taken a lesson myself, I think I have learned a lot, perhaps not about recipes but about a certain style of cooking and hospitality in Tuscany.

My job starts after lunch. It is a curious combination of work and pleasure that finishes feeling like a privilege. Every afternoon I take the fourteen participants over the hills of Chianti, down dirt track roads, through vineyards and olive groves with spectacular views of the countryside, to many of my favourite haunts. We wander through the tiny streets and piazza of a fortified medieval hamlet whose inhabitants have softened and brightened its stone walls with masses of flowering potted plants. We visit a gem of a Romanesque parish church, pure and simple, a splendid seventeenth-century villa with its lively baroque decorations and furniture still intact, and, along the way, stop to see local artisan food producers at work.

A week's sojourn at Coltibuono is schooling in itself. It was my home for five full years, and ten years later I am still learning from it. Life has been going on within its stone walls for nearly a millenium so it has a lot to teach. You learn to live in harmony with this accretion of history that has given it a unique life of its own or run the risk of incurring the ire of the resident ghosts, normally benevolent.

Coltibuono began life in the early eleventh century as a fortified Benedictine abbey, but prior to that a hospice for pilgrims on their way to Rome existed there, and 1000 years earlier the estate was the site of an Etruscan city, *Cetamura*, whose ruins are being excavated by a team of American archaeologists. It has been a private home since the mid-nineteenth century, after Napoleon expelled the monks and the property was bought by the family of Lorenza's husband. Now, in the monastic quadrangle where monks once strolled in silent meditation, you might have to dodge a grandchild or two racing around the corridors on their tricycles.

The cooking class participants sleep in bedrooms that were formerly monastic cells, gather in the family room with its vaulted ceiling and immense open fireplace, originally the medieval kitchen, party in the frescoed drawing room, the Renaissance refectory where the monks once ate and, in between the day's activities, relax in the cloister garden amid the scent of banks of lavender and Lorenza's roses.

I think most of the students find Lorenza herself a fascinating study. The mother and grandmother of four children, she is a strikingly beautiful woman with the blue-grey eyes of her Swiss mother and the dark complexion of her Neapolitan de'Medici ancestors, the princes of Ottaiano. Her simple charm and easy

Badia a Coltibuono in Chianti, home
for a week to participants in Lorenza
de'Medici's cooking classes.

grace disguise a more elusive and enigmatic personality. Then, of course, there is The Name, of which she makes light. It usually falls to me to fill in the family tree on the bus during our excursions and to bring out a skeleton or two from the closet.

In the kitchen there is much to learn from Lorenza besides recipes. In these days of food fanaticism it is particularly refreshing to find an accomplished, experienced and now even famous teacher for whom cooking is no big deal. This woman is no foodie, nor is she a 'let's have fun in the kitchen' type. For Lorenza cooking is simply a means to an end, and the end is the pleasure of enjoying a satisfying meal in the company of family and good friends. 'Simple', 'uncomplicated', 'elegant', 'refined', 'no last-minute fuss', are words you hear often during her classes. Like all persons of taste, she has very definite ideas about what is done and what is not done but takes her own opinion as well as other's with humour.

Every evening a group of Lorenza's friends and neighbours entertain her students in their homes. Each host is delightful and the house distinguished, a Renaissance villa, a splendid apartment overlooking the rooftops of Siena, a comfortably restored

Lorenza de'Medici demonstrates one of her primary culinary interests, seasoning with fresh herbs.

farmhouse, and the welcome is warm and friendly. The climax of the week, apart from the gala graduation supper celebrated with the traditional libations and valedictories, has always been, at least for me, dinner at Brolio Castle, where we are the guests of the Baroness Costanza and the Baron Bettino Ricasoli.

Brolio and the Ricasoli epitomize in a unique way the history and hospitality of Tuscany. The castle is the grandest in all the land, an immense, imposing red brick structure situated high on a hill at the strategic historic border between Florence and Siena. It commands a vast view that takes in at a glance the territory that once was the ancient fiefdom of the Ricasoli – Firidolfi family and in modern times their extensive wine estates. It was the nineteenth-century Baron Bettino Ricasoli, great grandfather of our host and second prime minister of the newly united Italy, who established the first legislation controlling the production of Chianti wine.

The present Baron and Baroness welcome our group to their magnificent country residence 'like important ambassadors of small nations', as one participant so aptly put it. An *aperitivo* of the estate's white wine is served on the terrace garden built atop the castle ramparts from where one can contemplate an unequalled panorama of Chianti unchanged for centuries. The Baron recounts the history of his family seat, from its medieval foundations through the interminable wars between Florence and Siena, the German occupation and the allied bombing, to more contemporary maintenance problems.

Eventually a servant tells the Baroness that dinner is served. We dine in the castle's great baronial hall, neo-gothic in style and cathedral-like in dimension,

Brolio Castle, ancestral residence of the Ricasoli-Firidolfi family for almost a thousand years.

decorated with medieval armour and seventeenth-century tapestries. We are seated with plenty of elbow room at an immense table that runs practically the entire length of the room. Each place setting would easily suffice for a family of four.

The Baroness describes the food as simple Tuscan country fare but it is prepared and served in a way fit for a baron. If pasta is served as a first course, it will be in the form of an elegant *timballo*, a baked mould with a fresh tomato sauce in the centre. The second course,

usually a colourful *involtini*, stuffed meat roll, or a fine *stracotto*, braised beef, is served on immense white platters surrounded by three or four vegetables, such as tender artichoke hearts, thinly sliced carrots, sautéed green beans and small, crisply toasted potatoes. Dessert might be a luscious home-made fresh fruit tart.

As the evening progresses I can observe from my vantage point at the end of the table how the gracious hospitality of our hosts and the abundant fine wines

Baroness Costanza and Baron Bettino
Ricasoli-Firidolfi in the dining hall of
Brolio Castle, about to receive guests
from Coltibuono, 'like important
ambassadors of small nations'.

of the house have eased the guests into feeling right at home in this awesome atmosphere. Some, I notice, seem to drift off into reveries all their own. A day that has begun in a medieval monastery and is drawing to a conclusion in a baronial castle is a taste of Tuscany not soon forgotten.

Menu for a Supper at Brolio Castle

TIMBALLO CON SALSA DI POMODORO
Baked pasta mould with mozzarella and tomato sauce

STRACOTTO
Chianti casserole

CROSTATA DI FRAGOLE
Strawberry tart

The mould is a way of getting around two rules of Italian gastronomic etiquette: never serve pasta at supper and do not dig into a bowl of spaghetti when you are eating at a castle. This *timballo* is elegant and sumptuous, yet uncomplicated in taste.

Stracotto means cooked extra-long and 'in good wine' is implied, in this case, Chianti from the Brolio estate. To give the castle effect it should be served sliced and arranged on a large white porcelain platter surrounded by three or four colourful sautéed vegetables by a servant with white gloves. If you do not have staff, hire one of the kids for the evening. The gloves are optional.

A fresh fruit tart is a perfect way to conclude a meal whose first two courses are quite substantial.

Right: Baked pasta mould with tomato and mozzarella sauce.

Timballo con Salsa di Pomodoro
BAKED PASTA MOULD WITH MOZZARELLA AND TOMATO SAUCE

Serves 6.
salt and pepper
1 tbsp/15 ml olive oil
10 oz/300 g *capellini* (very fine spaghetti)
3½ oz/100 g (7 tbsp) unsalted butter
1 egg, lightly beaten
2 tbsp freshly grated parmesan cheese
2 tbsp fine dry breadcrumbs
7 oz/200 g mozzarella cheese
2 oz/60 g Parma ham

SAUCE:
1 lb/2 kg fresh plum tomatoes
1 onion
1 clove garlic
3 tbsp extra-virgin olive oil
8 fresh basil leaves

Bring a very large saucepan of water to the boil. Season with 1 tablespoon salt and 1 tablespoon olive oil. Add the *capellini* and cook until just *al dente*.

Drain the pasta well and transfer it to a large bowl. Add half the butter, the egg and Parmesan cheese. Stir carefully and correct seasoning.

Butter a 2½ pint/1½ litre (6 cup) ring-mould and sprinkle it lightly with the breadcrumbs, shaking off any excess. Transfer half the pasta to the mould and dot the top with butter. Add the mozzarella and Parma ham and cover with the rest of the pasta. Press gently down with the palm of your hand. Dot with the remaining butter and sprinkle with the rest of the breadcrumbs.

A platter of braised beef and sautéed vegetables as served at Brolio Castle.

Meanwhile, make the sauce. Peel and roughly chop the tomatoes. Chop the onion and the garlic and saute in the olive oil until the onion is translucent. Add the tomatoes, season with salt and pepper and cook over moderate heat until the sauce has thickened. At the end stir in the basil leaves roughly torn.

Transfer to a preheated 375°F/190°C/Gas mark 5 oven and bake for about 25 minutes. Easing the sides with a knife, turn the mould onto a warm serving platter. Fill the centre with the tomato sauce, allowing it to overflow as this dish requires plenty of sauce. Decorate with a few sprigs of parsley or basil and serve immediately.

Stracotto
CHIANTI CASSEROLE

Serves 6.
6 fl oz/180 ml (¾ cup) extra-virgin olive oil
2 lb/1 kg chuck or stewing steak, cubed
1 yellow or red onion, finely chopped
2 carrots, peeled and finely chopped
1 celery stack, finely chopped
2 cloves garlic, finely chopped
8 fl oz/250 ml (1 cup) good quality Chianti
12 fl oz/350 g ripe tomatoes, peeled, seeded and chopped
5 fresh basil leaves, finely chopped
1 bay leaf
salt and pepper
1 pint/600 ml (2¼ cups) good beef broth

Heat the oil in a flameproof casserole. Add the meat and brown it over medium heat, taking care not to let it burn. Lower the heat add the onion, carrots, celery and garlic and cook, stirring occasionally, about 10 minutes, until the vegetables are soft.

A vaulted pergola covered by grape vine runs the full length and breadth of Lorenza de'Medici's garden at Coltibuono.

Raise the heat and stir in the wine, cooking and stirring until the wine has evaporated. Add the tomatoes with the basil and stir well. Season with salt and pepper. Add the bay leaf and 4 fl oz/125 ml (½ cup) beefstock. Bring to the boil, then lower the heat to a gentle simmer. Cover the casserole and leave to simmer gently for 2-3 hours, occasionally adding a little stock and stirring carefully.

Alternatively, the casserole may be placed in a preheated 325°F/170°C/Gas mark 3 oven for 2 hours.

Crostata di Fragole
STRAWBERRY TART

Serves 8-10.

PASTRY:
8 oz/250 g (2 cups) plain (all-purpose) flour
pinch salt
4 oz/125 g (1 stick) unsalted butter, cut up
1 tbsp/15 ml vegetable oil
cold water

FILLING:
1 284 g jar redcurrant jelly
grated rind (peel) of half lemon
10 oz/300 g fresh strawberries, hulled and halved if large
1 tbsp/15 ml caster sugar

Sift the flour with a pinch of salt onto a cool work surface. Make a well in the centre and put the butter and oil in it. Using your fingertips, gradually work the flour into the butter. If the mixture is too dry add 2 or 3 tablespoons cold water, but be careful not to add too much water as it toughens the pastry. Shape the

pastry into a ball, wrap in cling film (plastic wrap) and refrigerate for at least 1 hour.

Lightly butter a 10 in/25 cm loose-bottomed tart pan. Roll out the pastry and line the pan with it, making sure there are no cracks. Return the pastry case to the fridge for a further 30 minutes.

Meanwhile, melt the redcurrant jelly and stir in the grated orange rind peel. Leave to cool slightly. Remove the pastry from the refrigerator, prick all over with a fork. Transfer to a preheated 375°F/190°C/Gas mark 5 oven. Bake 16 to 18 minutes until golden brown.

Remove from the oven and arrange the strawberries in it. Sprinkle with a little caster sugar and brush with the lukewarm redcurrant jelly mixture. Return to the oven and bake for a further 7 minutes. Remove from the oven and leave to cool before serving.

A FEAST OF FISH ON THE ISLAND OF ELBA

I live in a land-locked province of Tuscany where fresh seafood is a rarity, even in restaurants. A fishmonger does visit my village every Thursday but as far as I can tell he never seems to do much business with the locals. Tuscans are a carnivorous folk. They also have the healthy instinct to want to know where their food comes from. Until recently most of them had tilled the land but many had never seen the sea. I once invited a neighbour to a nearby restaurant whose speciality is fish on Fridays. He ordered spaghetti with clams and ate all the spaghetti but left the clams in a little pile on his plate.

Two kinds of processed fish, however, have long been traditional Tuscan food. *Tonno sott'olio*, tuna preserved in olive oil, is prepared with white beans and red onions. *Baccalà*, salt dried cod, has been imported into Tuscany from Scandinavia since medieval times. It was a staple of the inland areas on the many days of religious abstinence from meat prescribed by the Church. Even in these less pious times my local store features *baccalà* every Friday, already soaked for twenty-four hours and ready to cook. In a dish called *baccalà alla fiorentina*, large chunks are fried and then stewed in tomato sauce.

Tuscans really prefer to wait until they are at the sea to eat fresh fish, and then they make a feast of it, ordering fish *antipasto*, fish on their pasta and fish, perhaps several kinds prepared in different ways, as the main course. The goal of a Sunday family outing is often a seafood meal on the coast. To get to their favourite fish restaurant Tuscans do not have very far to travel. A couple hours drive from even the furthest point inland will bring them to the shores of the Tyrrhenian.

The coastline of Tuscany stretches from the port and beaches of Massa-Carrara in the north, bordering on Liguria and the Italian Riviera, to the lovely promontory of Monte Argentário with its crowded, picturesque boat harbours at Porto Santo Stefano and Porto Ercole, some 400 kilometres to the south near Lazio and Rome. In the lagoon of Orbetello, between Monte Argentario and the mainland, fishermen trap *anguille*, common eels, as they return downstream to the sea from the Albegna river. They are prepared in a variety of ways, marinated in vinegar, smoked, stewed with onion and tomato sauce, grilled or roasted on skewers with bay leaves.

The region of Versilia in the north is the most popular section of the Tuscan coast. Its pride is the fashionable resort town of Forte dei Marmi. From its beaches you can look back at the Carrara marble quarries in the Apuan Alps that glisten like snow-covered peaks. Nearby are the more proletarian summer playgrounds of Camaiore and Viarèggio, where the season starts in late February with Viareggio's *Carnevale*, Europe's biggest Mardi Gras celebration.

Further down the coast is the major industrial port of Livorno, where *cacciucco*, the most famous Tuscan fish dish, originated. *Cacciucco alla livornese* is a fish soup so rich and thick that it is more like a stew. It belongs to the category of *zuppa*, a soup laddled over a slice of grilled (broiled) and garlic-rubbed bread. Originally it consisted of bits and pieces left over from that morning's market. Today you can ask your fishmonger to make the selection. The variety changes from village to village and from family to family but authentic *cacciucco* should include crustaceans and molluscs. My criterion for a good *cacciucco* is how many different kinds of seafood it contains.

Le Ghiaie, 'Pebble Beach', on Elba, not far from the island's main port and capital, Portoferraio.

(Sometimes the cook will cheat and put too much of one unpopular fish into the pot.) The soup is seasoned with parsley, garlic, tomatos, dry white wine and, most importantly, a generous pinch of the spice that gives *cacciucco* its particular savour, *zenzero*, the Tuscan word for *peperoncino* – chilli pepper.

From Livorno or further south from the smaller port of *Piombino*, the Pittsburg of Tuscany with more smoke stacks than San Gimignano has towers, you can catch a ferry boat for the Tuscan archipelago. The first time I set out to visit the islands I felt as if I were on a voyage of discovery. Islands in Tuscany? There are, in fact, seven principal ones besides a few rocky islets that rise out of the sea. Several are just names to me – and to most Tuscans. I had always assumed that Montecristo was somewhere off the coast of France, probably because the novel about its treasure and the Count had been written by Alexander Dumas. In reality, it lies about sixty kilometres from the Argentario. Montecristo is still practically inaccessible because of its steep contours and has become a national wildlife reserve. Pianosa is the Alcatraz of Tuscany. An ex-penal colony (like Gorgona, the northern most island in the archipelago), it has recently been renovated for the purpose of isolating convicted Mafia bosses.

Although I have made day trips to Giglio, Giannutri and Capraia, the island of Elba, the largest of the archipelago and after Sicily and Sardinia, the third largest of Italy, is the only island I visit regularly. Napoleon chose it as his home in exile 'because of its gentle inhabitants and mild climate'. The Siren that lures me to its shores is a restaurant that serves the most delicious fish dishes in all the Tuscan archipelago and well beyond.

From Piombino it is just a short hour's trip by ferry to Portoferráio, Elba's main port and capital of the island. The town is built on a promontory dominated by two forts constructed in the sixteenth and seventeenth centuries by the Grand Dukes of Tuscany to protect their interest in the island's rich iron-ore deposits. Fortified walls run right to the docks of the lively, industrious harbour. Ferry boats arrive from the mainland, mercantile ships are unloaded, pleasure craft and fishing boats line the wharf. The waters around Elba are rich in a great variety of fish and boats come from as far as the Bay of Naples to fill their nets. The local fishing industry, greatly diminished after the Second World War, is making a notable comeback and now has a fleet of over fifty boats.

Welcoming you as you enter through the city's grand central portal is a little shop under the arches that makes the best ice cream in Tuscany, according to a friend of mine well versed in these matters. Their chocolate topped with whipped cream gets a summer holiday off to a promising start. Inside the formidable walls the architecture of the old town is happily baroque and rococo, light, playful and pastel coloured The large, covered market hall has several stalls with fish still wriggling on the counters and offers a selection of locally grown fruit and vegetables, as well as produce from the mainland. Near the town hall there is a superior pizzeria whose speciality is chick-pea pizza.

Just outside Portoferráio at le Ghiaie, Pebble Beach, I know a small *pensione* of a kind that fortunately can still be found on the island. Each of its clean, sparsely furnished rooms has a tiny terrace looking down upon a crystal clear sea. On request the patroness will prepare dinner for her guests and to tempt you she will let you taste her seafood pasta sauces simmering on the family kitchen stove.

You could drive around Elba in several hours but it would take a few days to explore the immense variety of its sights and scenery. From the rocky peak of Monte Capanne, at an altitude of over 3,280 feet/1000 metres, you gain a vast and spectacular panorama of the island's jagged coastline and the other islands of the archipelago, with Corsica in the distance shrouded in mist. Ancient fortified towns, some untouched by tourism, stud hillsides covered with chestnut forests and almond groves. Winding along narrow roads you can glimpse small fishing villages with crescent-shaped beaches and at the bottom of sheer cliffs, sandy coves accessible only by foot down steep paths. Some of the villages are now resorts and flocks of mainland Italians and northern Europeans crowd the beaches during July and August. Yet, there is nothing glamorous nor glitzy about the island. Notwithstanding its beauty, part of Elba's charm is that it just misses being picture postcard precious.

On to that fish restaurant which is the goal of this outing to Elba. It is located in Capoliveri, an ancient island village high on a terraced hill on the southern promontory of the island with sweeping views of the coast below. By the coastal route it is a long drive from Portoferraio but luckily a cross-country shortcut can get you there in a hurry when you are hungry. The restaurant is called Il Chiasso, which means alley, and a narrow public passage up the steep incline of the village runs right through the premises. People passing by can peek through a little window into the kitchen, salute Claudio, the cook, and check on the day's menu. Built on different levels, the kitchen and dining rooms were originally stables carved into the hillside for the mules that were used to carry cargo up to the village and down to the sea.

One explanation for the origin of the name, Capoliveri, claims it is derived from the Latin, *caput Liberi*, headquarters of Bacchus. This interpretation fits in nicely with the local production of wine from vineyards that thrive in the iron-rich soil of the terraced slopes below the town. It also helps in describing the proprietor of Il Chiasso, Luciano Casini, who strikes me as a cross between Bacchus and Neptune. You can picture him emerging from the sea with a flask of wine in one hand and a big fish wiggling at the end of his trident.

Marciana, high in the hills of Elba, has terraced vineyards that slope down to a picturesque harbour.

A native of Capoliveri and the son of a fisherman, Luciano left the island to work in Germany, as did many of his contemporaries, and returned to Elba a few years later with his German wife, Dagmar. Like many of the best in his profession, he began the restaurant because he immensely enjoys eating good food and wanted to share his pleasure. I have watched him cook for friends at home and for clients in his restaurant and his high level of enthusiasm does not vary. Quite coincidentally *chiasso* also means hubbub and that describes the atmosphere of Il Chiasso. Locals drops by, regulars from the mainland arrive, English and German summer residents of the island return and Dagmar knows how to make everyone feel welcome.

I have a fundamental rule about how I like fresh fish cooked, the less you do to it the better, which erroneously led me to believe that the best one could hope for was a superior *spaghetti alle vongole* and a fine fish properly grilled (broiled). Luciano has broadened my horizons. He takes fish liver, for example, which is usually discarded, cooks it gently in butter with salt and pepper and adds a dash of Calvados. Foie gras of the sea, he calls it, and like that delicacy, it melts in your mouth. He also prepares a kind of goulash of the sea. Pieces of octopus are cooked in a base of white onions, garlic and rosemary, then potatoes are added and the ingredients left to simmer until tender. He serves pasta with a sauce he has named *sessuale*, sexy spaghetti, made from fish eggs simmered in olive oil, garlic and chilli pepper.

When Luciano goes to the fish market off the main piazza of Capoliveri, there is more talk about sex, specifically that of the *granceola*, spider crab, while he and the young fishmonger attempt to fish a few from a tank. The smaller female is considered better and will form the centrepiece of what is perhaps the masterpiece from his kitchen, a dish called *misto alla Luciano*, a kind of stew served on a large, deep platter with the cooked and cracked crab reassembled in the centre surrounded by pieces of a dozen different fish.

Luciano is partial to fine old Calvados to cleanse the palate between dishes. I prefer a cup of the delicious green apple sorbet that he brings over from the mainland.

The waters off Elba are rich in tuna and until recently migrating blue-fin tuna were diverted into the shallow waters around the Cape d'Enfola, not far from Portoferráio, trapped in nets and taken with gaffs, as fishermen still do in Sicily. Luciano uses fillets of fish tuna to make *involtini di tonno*, tuna rolls. Each fillet, with some anchovy, is wrapped in a lettuce leaf, laid on a bed of onions, topped with slices of green tomatoes and braised in white wine. *Acciughe*, anchovies, are another speciality of Elba. In the markets you see jars of anchovy fillets preserved in

Filleted fresh anchovies in the fish market at Portoferraio.

Spaghetti alla Luciano, a speciality of
Il Chiasso, is dressed with a
shellfish sauce.

olive oil. They are much better than the ones that come in cans. Fresh, they are even more delicious. My favourite way to eat them at Il Chiasso is as an *antipasto*, hot out of the pan, after the cook has dipped them in flour and fried them for a minute or two in olive oil.

A word of advice. In this kind of eating establishment, where the proprietor does the marketing, has a hand in the kitchen and attends to the guests, you should not order from the menu, but instead let him suggest the day's dishes. At the conclusion of the meal, Luciano might even be able to find a bottle of the rare local *Aleatico*, a rich, sweet red wine to complete the feast. It is said to have been Napolean's favourite during his stay on Elba.

Polpo con Patate
OCTOPUS WITH POTATOES

Luciano uses a small species of octopus and cooks it whole. It is more tender and requires less cooking than the larger species, which should be cut into pieces. Ask your fishmonger to clean and tenderize the octopus for you.

Serves 6.

3 cloves garlic
5 tbsp/75 ml olive oil
a few fresh sage leaves
1 sprig fresh rosemary
4 small octopus, cleaned and ready to cook
4 tomatoes, passed through a mouli-legumes or puréed
6 potatoes, peeled and roughly chopped
salt and pepper
dried chilli pepper to taste

Gently heat the whole garlic cloves in the olive oil in a large flameproof casserole. As soon as the oil is hot, add the sage, rosemary and octopus. Turn up the heat and stir vigorously, coating the octopus evenly in oil until the tentacles curl tightly back around the body and the garlic has taken on a light, golden colour.

Add the tomatoes and the potatoes and salt, pepper and chilli peppers to taste. Pour in enough water to almost cover the potatoes and simmer gently until these are tender. Turn off the heat and leave to stand for 20 minutes before serving.

Involtini di Tonno
FRESH TUNA FISH ROLLS

Luciano uses *ventresca di tonno*, tuna fish belly, the best part of the fish, for this simple, tasty dish. In good Italian food shops you can also buy it preserved in large tins, sold by weight.

Serves 6.
1 large head lettuce
1½lb/750g fresh tuna, preferably belly, cut into 1¾in/4cm cubes
6 anchovy fillets, halved
a handful of fresh basil leaves
4 cloves garlic, finely chopped
2 sweet, white onions, thinly sliced
4-5 tomatoes, preferably the long, San Marzano variety, thinly sliced
salt and pepper
dried chilli peppers, crushed to taste

Select the best medium-sized leaves from the lettuce and plunge them into warm water for a few seconds, then dry and lay them flat on a table or chopping board. Place a tuna cube in the centre of each leaf. Add ½ anchovy fillet to each, some basil leaves and a generous pinch of garlic.

Fold the leaves into little packets and fasten each with a wooden toothpick. Arrange them to cover the bottom of an oven-proof dish and cover with the onion belly and the tomatoes. Sprinkle with salt, ground pepper and chilli pepper. Drizzle generously with olive oil and place in a pre-heated 320°F/160°C/Gas mark 6 oven for 15 minutes. Let the dish stand for a further 15 minutes before serving.

Gifts from the sea, Luciano Casini, owner and chef of Il Chiasso, and his savoury fish soup.

Misto alla Luciano
LUCIANO'S FISH SOUP

This is Luciano's version of the traditional Tuscan fish soup, *cacciucco*. He does not pour it over bread but instead suggests you use the leftover sauce to dress a bowl of spaghetti and serve again right from the casserole.

This second dish he calls '*dolce del marinaio*' or 'sailor's pudding'.

Serves 6.
4 cloves garlic
1 bunch fresh parsley
3 chilli peppers
2½ fl oz/75 ml (⅓ cup) extra-virgin olive oil
6 fl oz/180 ml (¾ cup) white wine
1 800g can Italian tomatoes
a variety of small, flavourful fish, including some crustaceans and molluscs
½ tsp/2.5 ml dried oregano
½ tsp/2.5 ml marjoram
salt and pepper

Finely chop together the garlic, parsley and chilli pepper and gently sauté this mixture in the olive oil in a large flameproof casserole. When it begins to change colour add the wine, continue cooking to reduce and add the tomatoes.

Before the tomatoes begin to simmer add the pieces of cleaned fish and the crustaceans (if you use a lobster, split it in half).

Cover and cook over medium heat for 10 minutes. Then add the molluscs, cover and cook until their shells have opened, discard any which remain closed.

Add the oregano, marjoram, salt and pepper. Cook for a few more minutes, then serve.

ALFRESCO FESTIVALS

If you were to work it out right, you could eat at an outdoor *festa* in Tuscany practically every day from mid-June to mid-September, and at a cheaper price than it would cost to have dinner at home. These *feste* get underway with May Day celebrations and are in full swing by July. I am not referring to those festivals held in the larger towns and cities that feature medieval jousts and pageantry in Renaissance costume and attract crowds of spectators much to the delight of the tourist board.

What I am talking about are the small gatherings in the country that serve good *alfresco* food prepared by the locals and afterwards some dance music provided by more of the same. There are a few games of chance for both kids and adults and maybe a pizza stand where you can get a late night snack. These are affairs for families and friends and do not usually attract participants beyond the neighbouring villages. No re-enactment of historical events or arcane myths takes place here. *Feste* simply provide the Tuscan with an occasion to indulge his primeval appetite for eating, drinking and socializing in a congenial (and cool) atmosphere.

These convivial events fall into several categories. First of all there is the village *festa* pure and simple. This usually takes place on a weekend. The occasion might be the feastday of the patron saint. Originally many were grape harvest festivals now anticipated by a few weeks, since wine making has become serious business and the days of frolicking while stomping on grapes are long gone. Even in the smallest village these *feste* usually conclude with an impressive display of fireworks. At that moment the celebrating crowd, especially the children delighted to be up beyond their bedtime, move out of the well-lit piazza and into the vineyards and olive groves to watch the brilliant explosions high in a midnight-blue sky.

Then there is what might be called the political *festa*. One of the surest signs that summer is here to stay is when you begin to see red banners along the main street of a small town. These announce the *Festa dell'Unità*, the annual bash of the local Communist Party, now called the Democratic Party Of The Left. Since every village that has a party cell has a *Festa dell'Unità* staggered throughout the midsummer weeks, and since the majority of Tuscans has traditionally been of this political persuasion, these *feste* are the most numerous. Although they began as party fund-raising and recruiting events, today politics seems to be in the background and communal feasting to the fore. One thing is certain: everyone is welcomed. I have seen British nobility, German industrialists and American capitalists sit down at the same table with a group of comrades and nobody's appetite seemed to be adversely affected. Once, however, I did witness a protest demonstration at one of these *feste*. In those days it was common practice to use a live guinea-pig instead of a ball to play a kind of roulette game. The poor creature would be taken on a spin and whatever compartment of the revolving wheel he staggered into would be declared the winning number. A contingent from the local Radical Party, who had taken up the cause of these maltreated guinea-pigs, arrived on the spot and after a heated but non-violent confrontation succeeded in liberating the victim.

At both the village and political *feste* locals cook and serve. The selection of dishes is similar but the food at certain *feste* is superior. This is due to a purely fortuitous concentration that crosses party lines of especially talented cooks in a particular village. Word

Participants in the historical procession
that precedes Siena's Palio await the
arrival of the horses in the Piazza
del Campo.

gets around and those in the know will drive miles, passing by other *feste* in progress, to eat at one of these. I live right up the hill from a rather nondescript, not to say unattractive, place which, however, happens to have outstanding food at its *feste*. You have to line up early on the Friday night for the three-course feast of fish, a rare treat in this land-locked part of Tuscany.

Not surprisingly, the typical *festa* menu consists of the kind of food the villagers serve in their homes for family celebrations. To begin, there will be that most traditional of Tuscan *antipasti, crostini,* little rounds of crusty bread topped with a spread of chicken livers and *milza,* calf's spleen, cooked in white wine with

capers and garlic. As a first course the classic Tuscan bread and tomato soup, *pappa al pomodoro,* is popular. It is economical and practical to make in large quantities and can be served cold.

Food historians say pasta came late to Tuscany (some non-Tuscans would say *too* late) but *pappardelle sulla lepre,* an ancient regional speciality frequently featured at these *feste,* is a delicious dish of noodles second to none. *Pappardelle* are a wide ribbon pasta with ruffled edges traditionally dressed with pieces of hare (*lepre*) in a rich, thick sauce.

The main course is often composed of mixed roasted meats, chicken and guinea hen, *faraona,* are favourites. Mine is *arista,* roast loin of pork with garlic, fennel and rosemary, and if the *festa* is one of those superior events, a few slices might be included on the platter. Its perfect accompaniment, *fagioli,* Tuscan white beans, are almost always on the menu. You should beware the soggy salad but *patatine* are always a safe bet. Years ago my nieces and nephews, authorities on the subject, declared that Italians make the best chips (French fries) in Europe. It must be the olive oil.

For dessert I usually give the watermelon a miss and join the kids at the ice-cream stand for a truffle, choice of black or white, a cold confection that comes in chocolate or vanilla. If you pour a cup of hot espresso cafe over it, you have a *tartufo affogato,* a drowned truffle, and a fitting conclusion for a feast.

There are *feste* that are celebrated with food and then there are *feste* at which food is celebrated. These latter are called *sagre,* from the Latin *sacer,* meaning sacred. Cultural anthropologists say they got this name because they were originally held on the occasion of the consecration of a church. Others

Drummers and standard-bearers dressed in Renaissance costume wait on a side street before making their entrance onto the Piazza.

might say it is just another indication that food is sacred to Tuscans. These *sagre* abound throughout the season and their number seems to grow from year to year. You will see posters slapped against stone walls announcing *sagre* of everything from soup, *ribollita*, to nuts, *castagne*, with snails, frogs and wild boar inbetween. The only criterion seems to be, if it can be made to taste good, let's celebrate.

The format of these *sagre* is the same as for the other *feste* with the difference that the feted food is prepared and consumed in gigantic amounts. At a recent *sagra* of the snail, held annually in the small town of Cavriglia in the Valdarno, the buckets of this delicacy that had been prepared were not sufficient to satisfy the appetites of the masses that had gathered in its honour. By popular demand the township put on a *bis*, the Italian expression for 'we want MORE', the following weekend.

It may have occurred to the reader who is keeping count that the same village could conceivably have three different *feste*, at least. And indeed, many do.

In a category apart but still qualifying as a local *festa*, at least in atmosphere, are the outdoor meals the *contrade*, or wards, of Siena hold in their streets twice every summer, in July and August, on the evening before the *Palio*. Like everything connected with the *Palio* these good luck dinners are unique.

The *Palio* itself is a bareback horse race steeped in pageantry and hundreds of years of tradition. Ten of the city's seventeen *contrade*, chosen by lot, compete against each other. These wards function like small, independent states within the city. Each has its own governing body, church, meeting hall, social centre and museum, as well as insignia, usually an animal, colours, flag and anthem. More to the point, a complex and deeply felt network of animated alliances and rivalries has grown among them over the centuries. It is impossible, I think, for an outsider, even one who lives here, to fully understand let alone feel how profoundly the Sienese identify with their ward and the outcome of the *Palio* where the *contrade* vie for supremacy.

The objective is to win the race, of course, but it is just as important to work for the defeat of the enemy *contrada*. This constitutes a year-round endeavour: planning strategy, negotiating, secret diplomacy, securing a good jockey (riders are from outside Siena and, like mercenaries, sell themselves to the highest bidder) and organizing fund-raising events. Hun-

Andrea de'Gortes, nicknamed *Aceto*, 'Vinegar', wearing the colours of *Aquila*, the ward of the Eagle, waits for the starting signal. He went on to win his fourteenth Palio, a record for this century.

Tables set for the *Aquila* pre-Palio dinner follow the gentle curve of a street off the Piazza del Duomo.

welcomed as harbingers of good luck and even the passer-by may buy a seat at the table if any are still available.

These meals are also prepared and served by the locals, in this case, the *contradaioli*, members of the *contrada*. In the old days the women lowered tableware, as well as the food and drink, in baskets to the street from their apartment windows. Now the food is cooked in the well-equipped kitchens of the *contrada* social centre and the help of the professional chefs and restaurateurs of the ward is enlisted. During these occasions what one eats is definitely secondary to rallying enthusiasm for the next day's victory but the food is decent *festa* fare which amazingly, given the numbers and excitement involved, arrives at the table hot and with dispatch.

Over the years I have participated in many a good-luck dinner. Often my choice of venue is determined by considerations of such questionable patriotism as, which of the running *contrade* enjoys the most picturesque setting for its banquet, whose menu (published in the paper the day before) sounds the best and who is the odds-on favourite. Within recent memory I particularly recall a pre-*Palio* dinner of *Tartuca*, the ward of the tortoise. That year they had been alloted the best horse, had hired the best jockey and, since they had not won a *Palio* for a couple of decades, had a fierce determination to bring the victory banner home.

The long tables, enough for some 1400 *contradaioli* and their supporters, were set-up in the park-like piazza that runs parallel to the nave of the Renaissance church of Sant'Agostino. The area was festooned with the yellow and gold banners of the *contrada*, each with the symbol of a determined-looking tortoise.

dreds of millions of lire can be spent to manipulate a win that at the last minute can slip away by an act of fate, such as the allotment three days before the race of an inferior horse.

The week-long, pre-*Palio* excitement reaches its peak on the eve of the race. After the last of the evening trial runs that precede the day of the race, each participating *contrada* holds a dinner on a street or in a piazza within its territory. On that evening it is wonderful to wander through the winding, dimly lit, narrow streets of Siena and happen upon the spectacle of these brightly illuminated and somewhat boisterous banquets with several hundred participants at long cloth-covered tables. Guests are

Members of the *Aquila contrada* and
supporters rally enthusiasm during the
pre-Palio dinner.

The meal began merrily enough and as the courses were brought on the excitement mounted. We ate an *antipasto* of Sienese salami, a pasta of *crespelle alla senese*, pancakes (crêpes) stuffed with spinach and ricotta, *scaloppe*, thin slices of veal with *prosciutto* served with sautéed artichokes, and for dessert, individual portions of *zuppa inglese*, sponge cake soaked in liqueur and layered with custard. The young waiters and waitresses saw to it that our glasses were never empty of the Chianti furnished by a *protettore*, a *contrada* benefactor whose estate lies in the Sienese hills.

Frequently during the evening the youths of the ward seated together at special tables shouted out the ancient cadances of the *contrada* hymn whose words boast the virtues of the *Tartuchini* and disparage the arch enemy, the *Chiocciolini*, the members of the snail *contrada*, and more specifically, their respective sexual prowess. Increasingly their song took on the tone of a

battle hymn. It all built to a spectacular, if somewhat contemporary, conclusion. After enthusiastic pep talks to the cheering crowd by the *contrada* heads and a more cautious speech by the jockey, massive amplifiers blasted the William Tell overture accompanied by a rhythmic pounding of tables and stomping of feet. 'Hi! Yo! Silver'! And the next day the jockey, nick-named *Cianchino*, 'short-shanks', astride Uberto, a young bay gelding, won the *Palio* for *Tartuca*.

These *contrada feste* do not finish here. The members of the victorious contrada eat together every night for a month. Then, in September, there is a victory banquet at which the winning horse is the honoured guest, seated, as it were, at a special place behind the head table and fed a delicious dinner of oats and sugar. There are other celebratory feasts throughout the winter until it is practically time to begin the fund-raising dinners for the next *Palio*.

I once heard, but have been unable to verify, that it was formerly the custom at *contrada* meals to feature the heraldic animal, not its representation on a kind of decorated shrine as is done now, but on the plate – cooked. Presumably this practice was based on the theory that you are what you eat. Clearly, it was advantageous, from a purely gastronomic point of view, to have been born in the *contrada* of *Oca*, the goose, or even *Istrice*, the porcupine, rather than *Civetta*, the owl, or *Giraffa*, the giraffe, not to mention *Drago*, the dragon. At any rate, this may help to explain why *Bruco*, the caterpillar, through whose gates I enter the city of Siena (and therefore derive a sort of affiliation), has gone the longest within recorded memory, some thirty-five years, without winning a *Palio*.

Olive oil taking on the flavour of oregano, chili-pepper and bay leaf.

Menu for an alfresco Tuscan Festa Dinner

CROSTINI TRADIZIONALI
Chicken liver toasts

PAPPARDELLE SULLA LEPRE
Wide ribbon pasta with hare sauce

ARISTA AL RAMERINO
Roast loin of pork with rosemary and fennel

FAGIOLI ALL'UCCELLETTO
White beans and tomato

ZUPPA INGLESE
Italian trifle

This is sort of a fantasy *festa* menu. Although I have never been offered all these dishes at the same meal, I have eaten all of them, several times usually, during a season at various local *feste*.

The little toasts can be made without the spleen. I think they are best served warm. Dried *pappardelle* noodles, which are not inferior but merely different to fresh, are used at *feste*. Here grated Parmesan is not put on top of hare sauce. The roast loin of pork is cooked in the traditional Tuscan way, slowly, at low heat, so that all the fat has a chance to dissolve. The local *festa* cook who gave me the recipe for the beans recommends that they *not* be soaked before cooking to prevent them from becoming mushy. For the same reason she does not soak the ladyfingers for the *zuppa inglese* with Vin Santo but barely wets them.

Crostini Tradizionali
CHICKEN LIVER TOASTS

Makes 12.
4 tbsp/60 ml extra-virgin olive oil
½ small onion, finely chopped
1 small carrot, peeled and finely chopped
1 short celery stalk, finely chopped
1 tbsp/15 ml chopped fresh parsley
1 teaspoon grated lemon rind (peel)
pinch crushed dry mushrooms
5 chicken livers, cut in large pieces
3½ oz/100 g veal spleen, in large pieces
2 fl oz/60 ml (¼ cup) dry white wine
2 fl oz/60 ml (¼ cup) chicken stock
1 tbsp/15 ml capers, rinsed and chopped
2 anchovy fillets, drained and chopped
12 slices French bread, toasted

Warm the olive oil over medium heat in a frying pan (skillet). Add the onion, carrot, celery, parsley, lemon rind (peel) and mushrooms. Lower the heat and, stirring frequently, sauté until the onion is transparent. Add the livers and spleen, raise the heat and stir-fry about 5 minutes until the meat is brown. Add wine and cook for a further 3 minutes while scraping the bottom of the pan. Add the stock, lower heat and simmer very gently for about 20 minutes.

Put the mixture through the medium-sized disc of a food mill or chop finely, a food processor makes it too smooth. Add the capers and anchovies. Stir well to blend. Spread the mixture on the toasts and serve.

A platter of *crostini*, toasts with chicken liver spread, the most popular Tuscan *antipasto*.

Pappardelle sulla Lepre
PAPPARDELLE WITH HARE SAUCE

1 lb 3¼ oz/600 g hare or rabbit
4 tbsp/60 ml wine vinegar
4 tbsp/60 ml extra-virgin olive oil
3 oz/90 g unsmoked bacon, chopped
2 cloves garlic, peeled and chopped
2 small onions, chopped
2 celery stalks, chopped
1 carrot, peeled and chopped
3 plum tomatoes, peeled and diced
1 oz (30 g) (½ cup) chopped flat Italian parsley
5 fresh sage leaves
2 tbsp chopped fresh rosemary
1 clove
pinch grated nutmeg
salt and freshly ground black pepper to taste
12 fl oz/350 ml (1½ cups) good quality Chianti
4 fl oz/125 ml (½ cup) beef stock

If using hare, marinate it overnight in the wine vinegar mixed with water to cover. The next day, drain, dry and divide the hare into fairly large pieces. Heat the oil in a saucepan. Add the hare and brown over medium heat. Remove the hare, lower the heat and add the bacon, garlic and onions. Sauté gently about 4 minutes until the onion is transparent. Add the vegetables, herbs, spices and seasoning. Sauté gently for 5 minutes. Return hare to the pan, add half the wine and all the broth. Stir well, lower the heat and simmer gently, covered, for about 1½ hours. During this period gradually add the remaining wine.

Remove the hare from the sauce and bone it. Cut the meat coarsely and return it to the sauce, adding a little wine or broth if the sauce seems too dry. Adjust the seasoning.

Meanwhile, bring a large pan of salted water to the boil, add pasta and cook until *al dente*. Drain the pasta well and turn onto a warm serving dish. Cover with the sauce and serve at once.

Arista al Ramerino
ROAST LOIN OF PORK

Serves 6.
3 cloves garlic
1 tbsp/15 ml fresh rosemary spiked
4 leaves fresh sage
½ tbsp/7.5 ml fennel seed
2 kg/4 lb loin of pork
salt
4 tbsp/60 ml extra-virgin olive oil

Chop the garlic, rosemary and sage together. Mix in the fennel seed. Fill a larding needle with the mixture and, at the centre of the meat, run it through the full length of the roast. Otherwise make several incisions in the meat and stuff them with the mixture. Rub all over with salt first, then with olive oil.

Right: Fresh *pappardelle*, are cut with a fluted pastry wheel into their traditional shape.

Pour the rest of the oil into a roasting pan and place the roast in it with the fat side up. Transfer to an unheated oven set at 400°F/200°C/Gas mark 6. As soon as it reaches this temperature, reduce the heat to 325°F/170°C/Gas mark 3. Roast for about 1½ hours, turning twice during the cooking period.

Fagioli all'Uccelletto

WHITE BEANS AND TOMATO

Serves 6.
1 lb/500 g dried cannellini beans, or Great Northern beans
6 tbsp/15 ml extra-virgin olive oil
3 cloves garlic
10 fresh sage leaves
salt and pepper
1 onion, finely chopped
1 small carrot, peeled and finely chopped
1 celery stalk, finely chopped
2 tbsp/30 ml chopped fresh flat Italian parsley
1 lb/500 g plum tomatoes, peeled and chopped

Rinse but do not soak the beans. Transfer the beans to a large flameproof casserole. Add 2 tablespoons olive oil and cover with cold water. Over very low heat, bring the beans to the boil as slowly as possible. Add the garlic and sage and season with salt and pepper. Lower the heat, cover and simmer very gently about 1½ hours until the beans are soft but not mushy.

Meanwhile, in another flameproof casserole large enough to hold the beans, heat the remaining oil. Add the onion, carrot, celery and parsley. Sauté over low heat for about 3 minutes. Add the tomatoes, stir and leave to cook gently for about 10 minutes. Transfer the cooked beans to the tomato mixture, stir well, adjust the seasoning and cook for a further 10 minutes.

Zuppa Inglese

ITALIAN TRIFLE

Serves 6.
16 fl oz/500 ml (2 cups) milk
4 egg yolks
2 tbsp/30 ml sugar
2 tbsp/10 ml plain (all-purpose) flour
7 oz/200 g lady fingers
4 fl oz/125 ml (½ cup) Vin Santo mixed with an equal amount cold water

Heat the milk until very hot but not boiling, then remove from the heat. Beat the egg yolks in a bowl and gradually add the sugar, beating about 3 minutes, until the mixture is pale and thick. Gradually beat in the flour, making sure there are no lumps. Very slowly stir in the milk and continue stirring until well blended. Return the mixture to the saucepan.

Stand the saucepan over a pan of boiling water and, over medium heat, stir constantly until the sauce is slightly thick and smooth. Take great care not to let the sauce boil. Remove the saucepan from the heat and pour the sauce into a bowl. Stir for a couple of minutes, cover and allow to cool completely.

Dip the lady fingers very quickly into the Vin Santo. Line the bottom of a glass bowl with a layer of lady fingers and cover with the custard. Continue making layers until the ingredients are used up, but finish with the custard. There should be 3 or 4 layers, depending on the size of the bowl. Chill slightly before serving.

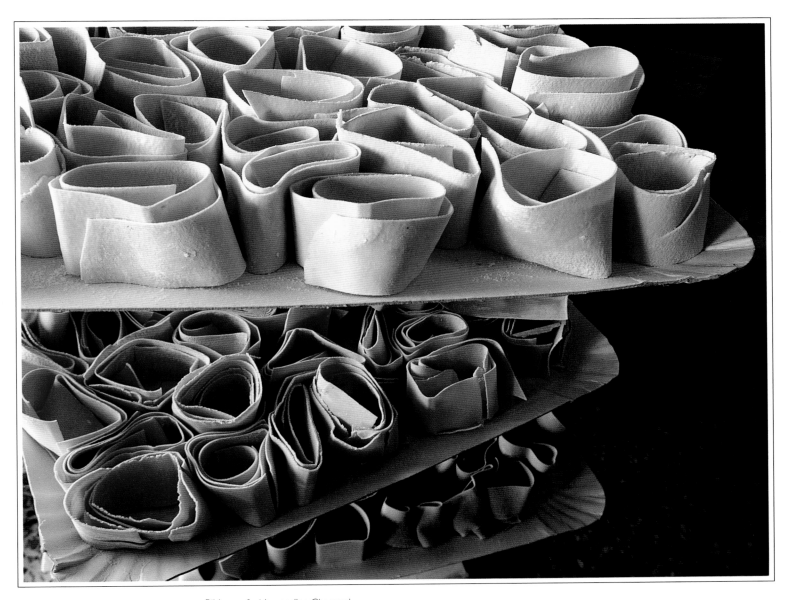

Ribbons of wide noodles. Chopped
spinach is sometimes added to the
dough for green lasagne.

AUTUMN

It always takes me by surprise. One day, usually in late September, you wake to a certain snap in the air. The atmosphere is translucent after weeks of summer haze. The colours of the landscape are in sharp contrast, an almost spring green in the fields and in the woods the leaves are turning brilliant yellow. Autumn has arrived.

CHESTNUT GATHERING & MUSHROOMING NEAR LUCCA

t always takes me by surprise. One day, usually in late September, you wake to a certain snap in the air. The atmosphere is translucent after weeks of summer haze. The colours of the landscape are in sharp contrast, an almost spring green in the fields and in the woods the leaves are turning brilliant yellow. Autumn has arrived.

The weather begins to cool and the days grow perceptibly shorter. We seem to spend more time at table, prolonging *alfresco* luncheons to soak in the last warm rays of the sun and enjoying longer suppers before the comforts of a fire. In Tuscany this is the season of plenty, and you need time simply to taste the abundance of nature's gastronomic grand finale before she settles down for a long winter's nap. In many ways the best has been saved for the last and like the brightly coloured leaves, their season will pass all too quickly. Now we have sweet chestnuts, mushrooms of eccentric shape and weird colours, rare white truffles, luscious late-season tomatoes, grapes, purple figs, juicy berries, pumpkin-coloured persimmons and the first small game birds to spit-roast on the fire.

The best place in Tuscany I know for savouring this season is Lucca and the Lucchesia, its surrounding area. There is something about the city of Lucca that is like autumn itself, genial and mellow. It has neither the formality of Siena, nor the harshness of Florence. Walking through the streets of Siena you are obliged by the high gothic buildings to strain your neck. In Florence you hardly dare look anywhere but straight ahead to manoeuvre safely through the traffic on sidewalk and street.

In Lucca life is lived at a leisurely pace. You can stroll down narrow streets that still follow their original Roman plan without fear of being run down by cars or rushing Lucchesi. Its Romanesque churches and Renaissance palaces are congenial and friendly. The fourteenth-century *Palazzo Guinigi* even has a sense of humour. It grows a little grove of ilex trees at the top of its tall, red-brick tower. Every hundred paces or so the streets open up to small, hospitable squares, many enlivened by a colourful marble façade and often a comfortable café.

The most marvellous of these are the splendid piazza and enchanting white limestone church of San Michele. This is the heart of Lucca. It was the site of the ancient Roman Forum, and today children and dogs play peacefully in the square until well after dark under a golden light from ancient wrought-iron lanterns. Medieval houses, renaissance palaces and a delightful arched loggia surround the piazza. There are a couple of good cafés and the pastry shop of Mario Taddeucci makes particularly tasty *buccellato*, a sweet bread speciality of Lucca. In the shape of a ring, it is studded with raisins and flavoured with aniseed.

From the apex of his church a sturdy Archangel Michael commands the scene below. Very much the triumphant warrior he was reputed to be he stands with wings spread and satan in the form of a huge serpent slain by his spear well under heel. He is flanked by two lesser principalities blowing their horns in victory. They stand atop a fantastic four-tiered façade of romanesque arcades that rise high above the nave. These are inlaid with birds and animals in perpetual motion and each arch is supported by a series of multi-coloured, ornately sculptured columns. It is a work of art that never ceases to delight the eye.

Notwithstanding its medieval and Renaissance

A circular row of houses built on the
foundations of Lucca's Roman
amphitheatre maintains its
original shape.

Above: Di Simo, the favourite café of photographer John Ferro Sims in Lucca. *Right:* From the apex of his church on Lucca's central piazza, Archangel Michael keeps a watchful eye on the scene below.

buildings, there is a late nineteenth-century feel about Lucca. During a *passeggiata* along *via Fillungo*, 'the way of the long thread', that runs through the centre of the city, you pass numerous little shops whose *art nouveau* fronts have miraculously survived intact. Even though what they sell inside has sometimes changed, the owners have had the good sense and taste to leave the beautiful old lettered glass signs in place. About midway along this street I like to stop for a drink at Di Simo, as unchanged and charming as it must have been when Lucchese café society was flourishing.

A few minutes' drive outside the red brick Renaissance ramparts that perfectly encompass the city will take you into the surrounding hills where,

beyond the olive groves and villas, you enter forests of immense chestnut trees. On fine, mid-October mornings chestnut gathering in these woods is a popular family recreation. If you have the good luck to arrive on the very day when the prickly burrs first begin to open, you can hear the reddish brown nuts fall to the ground and begin to wonder whether you should have brought along a helmet. Try to get there before the wild boar whose favourite food they are.

The kind of chestnuts to look for are called *marroni*, the fruit from a variety of chestnut tree that has been grafted on to the rootstock of the common *castanea sativa* and is cultivated in the mountainous regions of Tuscany. *Marroni* are large, plump, bright in colour and flavourful. They also have a thinner shell and inside skin which makes they easier to eat. Ordinary chestnuts are thrown to the pigs, while fresh *marroni* cost about 8000 lire a kilo.

Only in the late twentieth century has chestnut gathering become a pleasant pastime. In less prosperous periods, especially during wars when food was particularly scarce, peasants gathered them to survive. The people who lived in the poor, remote,

Marroni chestnuts, some still in their prickly burrs, are gathered from the ground and will be roasted, boiled or ground into flour.

mountainous regions of Tuscany ground the nuts into a fine, soft, dusty white flour that they used for making bread and polenta. In the Garfagnana, an area north of Lucca, mills still grind chestnuts into this sweet flour.

Nowadays, you are most likely to taste the flour in an unusual cake called *castagnaccio*. The fresh chestnut flour is mixed with water and olive oil, seasoned with raisins, pine nuts, fennel seeds and often rosemary and baked in a round, shallow, copper pan. The result is a kind of semi-sweet flat bread. Many old recipes say it should be cooked until it has the appearance of 'parched earth', brown and cracked. On the inside it is a curious pink colour and has the consistency of pudding.

Bakeries sell *castagnaccio* by the piece, and, although I have never really acquired a taste for this sweet, I always try at least one seasonal slice. When you eat it hot, washed down with a glass of *novello*, new wine with a light, natural sparkle, as they serve it at the Cantinetta Antinori in Florence, it is even convincing.

There are a couple of country festivals that celebrate the season with other sweets made from chestnut flour. In Pontremoli, a town of the Lucchesia, they make *necci*, chestnut flour pancakes (crêpes). The batter is cooked over hot embers on an ancient implement called a *testi*, which consists of two iron disks at the end of long handles, and is filled with fresh ricotta or *pecorino* cheese. At Marradi in the province of Florence, they eat *polentine dolci*, slices of sweet polenta made from chestnut flour.

Chestnut season today is an occasion for family and friends to spend time together round the fire on the first chilly evenings of autumn. Roasting chest-nuts seems to be to contemporary country life what popping popcorn and roasting marshmellows were to my American youth, except chestnuts are much tastier, more nutritious and according to Mattioli, a sixteenth-century Sienese doctor, an aphrodisiac as well.

The ritual of roasting chestnuts is performed by means of another long-handled instrument. This one has a round iron pan at the end with holes punched into the bottom. Before they go into the pan, the plump *marroni* are 'castrated', as they say around here, their shell and inner skin slit with a knife along the width of the round side to facilitate peeling once they are roasted. Then they are tossed over the fire until their shells begin to burn and burst. In Chianti roasted chestnuts are called *bruciate*, burnt, and in Florence, *caldarroste*, hot-roasted.

Sometimes, instead of roasting, the nuts are boiled in water with a pinch of fennel seeds. A dish of these is called *ballotte* in some parts of Tuscany and *ballocciori*, in the Lucchesia. In Florence street venders roast chestnuts in portable braziers and sell them wrapped in heavy paper cones. Their aroma warms the atmosphere and they provide an excellent quick energy snack for combating city crowds.

When the late autumn wind and frost detach the dried, oblong leaves of the chestnut tree, they fall to the ground and form a thick carpet in the woods that becomes a mouldy mulch for next year's mushrooms. The season for wild mushrooms in Tuscany can begin as early as late spring but it is the humidity of early autumn, when the combination of heat and rain *'fa bollire la terra'*, makes the earth boil, that produces heaps of mushrooms. Some seasons there are virtually none due to lack of rain or early frost. Other times there are just a few. Then there are years like this when bumper crops keeps popping up well into November.

Whereas gathering chestnuts may be a pleasant pastime for some, mushrooming is a passion of the masses. When word gets around town that the first mushrooms of the season have been found, carpenters, plumbers, car mechanics and housewives declare a holiday and head for the woods. On the weekends the city folk follow. Their cars line country roads from Lucca in the north to Arezzo in the south.

The professionals are the locals. Each has their secret section of the woods where they have struck it rich before. Some are acknowledged by the others as having a sixth sense for spotting prime specimens that no one else can see, sort of like sighting gnomes. A certain woman from my village, said to be endowed with this power, sets out before sunrise to avoid being followed to her haunts.

The species of mushroom everyone is searching for above all others is the *Boletus*, in Italian, *porcini*, so called, I would imagine (no one seems to be sure),

Handsome specimens of the *boletus edulis*, *porcini*, the most sought after mushroom of the Tuscan countryside.

because of its fat, squat shape. Anna Marrocchi, my neighbour and the woman who does *not* come to clean my house during the height of the season, keeps me up to date with periodical *porcini* reports and occasionally a finding for my supper. 'Today we came back with four kilos,' she tells me, just average in a good year for a few hours spent scrabbling about on hands and feet in the woods. On her best day this year she brought back 20 pounds/ten kilos of *porcini*. Around here there are no laws limiting the quantity you can pick. In areas where people make a living hunting wild mushrooms the maximum is 4 pounds/ two kilos a day per person.

Not only Anna but all her family and relations are real pros at this 'sport'. They set out in their cars wearing boots and bring along walking sticks and large baskets woven from strips of chestnut wood. The baskets have a hard, thick, arched handle that they use for support while they are climbing along hillsides and crawling through the underbrush.

These intrepid hunters do not limit their vision to *porcini*. At least half a dozen or so other edible mushrooms grow in the Tuscan woods, including several varieties of the *Boletus*. My favourite is the rare and exquisite *ovolo*, egg-mushroom, botanically *Amanita caesarea*. When they are young, *ovoli* are completely enclosed in an egg-shaped and egg-coloured volva that opens later to reveal a beautiful yolk-orange cap. They are of the same *Amanita* family as the dreaded Death Cap, but fortunately not blood relations. *Ovoli* are always eaten raw and are superb sliced and mixed with shavings of fresh Parmesan dressed with olive oil and lemon.

Back in Anna's kitchen, where she keeps a large framed poster depicting the most important members of the mushroom family, Anna cooks, dries, preserves and, in an abundant year, even freezes her *porcini*. She discovered several years ago that frozen *porcini* maintain their aroma and flavour perfectly (which I can verify) and bought a second freezer specially for them. She wipes the *porcini* clean, bags them both whole and sliced and only partially thaws them under running water before she grills (broils), fries and uses them to season her sauces all year round.

For years I entertained a recurring day-dream in which I was proprietor of a successful farmhouse restaurant in Tuscany. The food, everyone agreed, was marvellous and the hospitality perfect. I varied the details of this fantasy but the constant image was of tables on a sunny terrace overlooking a spectacular view, where the herb and vegetable garden grew right up to the toes of my contented guests. Another particular I never changed: the farmhouse was always painted an old, washed-out burnt rose.

Then, several years ago, I discovered that this restaurant of my dreams actually existed and no further away than a short drive into the hills outside the city of Lucca. It has, in fact, been there for several hundred years, although it only began to assume the shape of my dream during the last thirty, when Rosa and Pietro Casella turned an old roadside inn and farmhouse into a restaurant. It is their son, Cesare, who has brought my fantasy to fulfillment.

The restaurant is called Vipore, which means vipers and there is a bas-relief of these deadly serpents right outside the front entrance. The story goes that the old innkeeper used them to warm the bed of guests who gave him any trouble. I look upon them as the sacred protectors of the treasure inside.

Vipore is not easy to find. You must follow in blind faith an unmarked back road that winds up into hills of terraced olive groves and vineyards, then through a wood until you come to the rose-coloured building. Once there, you immediately get the feeling that this is the kind of eating establishment where you will want to settle-in for a while. One autumn day I arrived with a couple of friends about 1 pm and we did not leave until 7 pm, seven bottles of wine and at least as many different dishes later.

We did, however, take a couple of breaks from the table to walk in Cesare's garden that grows right up to the terrace. Here he cultivates over forty species of

Cesare Casella, chef of Vipore, relaxes at his private table overlooking Lucca.

herbs. In some spots he lets them grow with abandon, in others he has disciplined them into rock lined beds at the feet of gnarled old olive trees. He uses most of them in the kitchen. Cesare's dishes are uncomplicated, rooted in the tradition of the countryside and cooked with skill: a plate of thinly sliced pork fat (fatback) with crushed peppers and served with hot, lightly grilled bread into which it melts like the creamiest of butter; *zuppa di gran farro*, a soup made with a barley-like grain with a rich, nutty taste; *uova e carne secca del Pontormo*, an antipasto salad of scrambled eggs, greens and salami, created by Cesare after he had read that the sixteenth-century Tuscan artist, Pontormo, was fond of a similar concoction.

And speaking of *porcini* mushrooms, Cesare prepares them in at least fifteen different ways: in salads, soups, pastas, *frittate*, deep fried, sliced and sautéed with the herb that is their most congenial companion, *nepitella*, wild mint, and preserved in olive oil with bay, chilli peppers and garlic. A favourite of mine is a dish of fried polenta *crostini* topped with a *porcini* sauce and served on parchment paper.

There are many rooms in the Casella hilltop haven, kitchens centred around a large fireplace for roasting and grilling squab, rabbit, lamb, veal, pork and huge rib steaks of beef, a spacious dining-room, a bar with tables that Cesare keeps free for neighbours and friends, and a small store where he sells all the ingredients of a hearty picnic for the chestnut-gatherers and mushroom-hunters who pass this way.

One table Cesare reserves for himself. It sits, solitary, at the end of a grassy knoll that extends like a penisola from the terrace of the restaurant. The view from here is spectacular. On one side are the hills of the Lucchesia studded with ancient churches and villas and on the other, down in the distance, the towers of Lucca, that seem so close on some days you could touch them. He retires to this table with a favourite bottle of wine ('and never more than two glasses') to wind down after a day's work and, one would imagine, to plan the next day's activities.

Cesare gives the impression of being a young man with an agenda, full of energy, curious and well informed about what goes on in his profession. He makes frequent forays across the border to France and travels to America in the winter, bringing along a solid, critical sense. Unlike his Imperial namesake, whom he might be said to resemble with curly black beard and aquiline nose, in zany plaid trousers instead of toga, he is not out to conquer the world. Cesare is definitely aware of what he already has, a restaurant that is a dream come true.

Insalata di Funghi Porcini
— PORCINI SALAD —

Cesare Casella's simple salad is the most delicious way I know for enjoying fresh raw *porcini*. If you cannot find any *boletus edulis*, try substituting another species of a firm, solid wild mushroom.

Serves 6.
2 tsp/10 ml salt
2 tbsp/30 ml lemon juice
2 tsp/10 ml freshly ground black pepper
1 tbsp/15 ml finely chopped flat Italian parsley
½ tbsp/15 ml finely chopped *cala* or ordinary mint
4 fl oz/125 ml (½ cup) extra-virgin olive oil
12 oz/350 g small *porcini* mushrooms
4 oz/125 g mixed rucola (rocket/arugola), Cas (romaine) and curly lettuce, shredded
2 oz/6 g Parmesan cheese

Dissolve the salt in the lemon juice. Add the pepper and chopped herbs and gradually whisk in the oil until well blended.

Clean the mushrooms with soft brush or wipe them with a damp cloth. Cut the mushrooms lengthways into very thin slices. Arrange the mixed greens on a flat serving dish and dress it with a little of the oil and lemon. Cover the salad with the sliced mushrooms and sprinkle with the rest of the salad dressing. Using a swivel-bladed potato peeler, shave the Parmesan cheese over the mushrooms. Serve at once.

Plate of *porcini* salad on a bed of mint.

Uova e Carne Secca del Pontormo
— PONTORMO BACON AND EGGS —

Cesare Casella got the inspiration for this simple, tasty dish late one night when he read that the sixteenth-century Tuscan painter, Pontormo, was fond of a similar snack. At Vipore it is served as an *antipasto* but it is perfect for a savoury brunch.

An artistic dish of bacon, eggs and greens named after the painter, Pontormo.

Serves 4.
½ tsp/2.5 ml salt
2 tbsp/30 ml wine vinegar
½ tsp/1.25 ml black pepper
4 fl oz/125 ml (½ cup) extra-virgin olive oil, plus 1 tbsp/
15 ml
4 oz/125 g (rocket/arugla), dandelion or other small leaf
salad leaves, shredded
4 oz/125 g bacon (slab bacon), in julienne strips
1 tbsp/15 ml finely chopped fresh basil, parsley and
chives, mixed
8 eggs, lightly beaten

Dissolve the salt in the vinegar. Add the pepper, then slowly whisk in the 4 fl oz/125 ml (½ cup) olive oil. Check seasoning and add the salad leaves. Toss lightly.

Heat 1 tablespoon olive oil in a frying pan (skillet). Add the bacon and herbs and fry until the bacon is just crisp. Remove the pan from the heat and add the eggs. Return the pan to low heat and stir gently until the eggs are soft and moist. Remove the pan from the heat immediately and transfer the scrambled eggs to the salad bowl. Toss well and serve at once.

Tuscan bean and Luccese grain soup.

Gran Farro della Garfagnana

TUSCAN BEAN AND GRAIN SOUP

Gran farro, emmer in English, is a dark, barley-like grain with a rich, nutty, autumnal flavour and a firm consistency. This soup is native to the Lucca region, especially popular in the area of the Garfagnana. This is how it is prepared at Vipore.

Serves 4-6.
12 oz/350 g (2 cups) dried red kidney beans
12 oz/350 g (2 cups) emmer, well rinsed
pork knee bone or ham bone
2 garlic cloves
3 oz/90 g unsmoked bacon (slab bacon), chopped
½ tbsp/7.5 ml fresh rosemary spikes, chopped
4 fresh sage leaves
salt and pepper
2 onions, chopped
2 celery stalks, chopped
1 large carrot, peeled and chopped
1 leek, chopped and well rinsed
4 fl oz/125 ml (½ cup) extra-virgin olive oil, plus extra
for serving
Tabasco sauce, to taste
3 small potatoes, peeled and diced
6 oz/180 g can tomato purée (paste)
4 fl oz/125 ml (½ cup) dry white wine

Leave the dried red kidney beans to soak in water to cover overnight. Drain the beans and transfer them to a large stockpot. Add 4½ pints/2.5 litres (2½ quarts) water, the bone, garlic, bacon, rosemary and sage. Bring to the boil for 10 minutes over medium heat, then skim the surface and leave to boil for about 40 minutes. Season with salt and cook for a further 10 minutes.

In another large pan gently sauté the onions, celery, carrot and leek in the olive oil. Add the Tabasco sauce, pepper, potato, rosemary and tomato puré (paste). Stir well and cook for a further 5 minutes. Add the white wine and leave it to evaporate for a further 5 minutes.

Add the emmer to the pan. Set aside ¾ pint/500 ml (2 cups) stock and add the contents of the bean pan with the emmer. Leave to cook for about 50 minutes, adding the reserved stock if necessary. Serve with a little extra-virgin olive oil for spooning over each serving and freshly ground black pepper.

Walnuts are sometimes sprinkled on top of the traditional chestnut flour cake.

Castagnaccio
CHESTNUT FLOUR CAKE

I read a sixteenth-century reference to this rustic sweet written by a monk from Lucca. All the old recipes say it should be baked until the crust is brown and cracked like parched earth. It tastes best served warm with a glass of sweet Vin Santo.

Serves 6–8.
12 oz/350 g (3 cups) chestnut flour
5 tbsp/75 ml extra-virgin olive oil, plus extra 1 tbsp/15 ml for pan
3 oz/90 g (½ cup) seedless raisins
3 oz/90 g (½ cup) pine nuts
2 tbsp/30 ml coarsely chopped fresh rosemary
pinch of salt

Soak the raisins in lukewarm water for about 30 minutes, then drain well and set aside.

Sift the chestnut flour into a large bowl. Gradually add 12 fl oz/350 ml (2½ cups) water and 5 tbsp olive oil, stirring constantly to prevent lumps from forming. Stir in half the pine nuts and the raisins into the fairly liquid mixture.

Grease an 11-inch/27.75 cm cake tin with 1 tbsp/7.5 ml olive oil. Pour in the mixture. Sprinkle with the remaining pine nuts and olive oil. Top with chopped rosemary. Bake in an oven preheated to 400°F/200°C/Gas mark 6 for about 40 minutes. Remove the pan from the oven and shake off any excess olive oil. Transfer the cake to a plate and serve.

WINE MAKING IN CHIANTI

Chianti, the best-known wine of Italy, is practically synonymous with Tuscany. Before it was the name of a wine, however, Chianti referred to a territory between Florence and Siena that in medieval times comprised the area around the towns of Gaiole, Radda and Castellina in south-central Tuscany, now part of the province of Siena. In those days this terrain was hotly and constantly contested between Florence and Siena who both wanted, among its other advantages, all the wine for themselves.

Long before the Middle Ages, wine was already being produced in this area. The Etruscans were the first to cultivate vines on its slopes. In fact some scholars hold that the word 'Chianti' is Etruscan in origin. Vines trained on trees, an Etruscan method of viticulture, can still be seen bordering patches of farmland along country roads. The Romans pretty much wiped-out the Etruscans and their civilization but they kept the vines and expanded the vineyards to surrounding areas, as did medieval feudal barons and monks, Renaissance landlords and the gentry of the eighteenth century.

As a result, production of the wine that gradually came to be called Chianti spread far beyond its place of origin, until limits were finally set to the area that could produce Chianti in the early twentieth century. These boundaries include a vast territory covering the central hills of Tuscany, stretching almost to the sea at Pisa, that is divided into seven zones: Chianti Classico, Colli Fiorentini, Rufina, Montalbano, Colli Aretini, Colli Senesi and Colline Pisane.

Today the word 'Chianti' primarily refers to the wine. In the countryside between Florence and Siena, however, roughly the production zone of Chianti Classico, the inhabitants, using their ancient historical prerogative, say they are from Chianti and are known as *chiantigiani*.

Over the years I have heard many a well-travelled visitor exclaim that Chianti Classico is the most beautiful wine country in the world. Happily vineyards have not taken over the terrain. Olive groves and large wooded areas alternate with vines on hills crested with rows of cypress, interspersed with medieval castles, fortified hamlets, Renaissance villas and ancient stone farm houses. It is a landscape both wild and cultivated, rustic and civilized.

The wine is as varied as the terrain on which it is produced. Traditionally, in accordance with a formula established since the late nineteenth century, Chianti was a blend of four grapes, two red varieties, Sangiovese and Canaiolo Nero, and two whites, Trebbiano Toscano and Malvasia del Chianti. What might seem a profanity, adding white grapes to red wine, was done to soften the dominant red San-giovese, a firm, robust variety with high tannin content. Producers wanted to make their Chianti drinkable without ageing it for a local market that preferred a young, light wine.

Recent regulations have reduced the minimum of white grapes in Chianti Classico to 2 per cent. Many producers interpret the law as permission to leave them out altogether. The fact is, wine-makers who wanted to make a Chianti with bigger body and greater ageing potential had been omitting white grapes from their vintages since the early 1980s. The new regulations also allow the addition of a maximum 10 per cent of other red grapes to the Chianti formula.

This flexibility of the traditional formula, together

Wooded areas alternate with
vineyards in Tuscany's Chianti Classico
wine region.

with improved methods in vineyards and cellars introduced by a new generation of winemakers (often university-trained oenologists and viticulturists) and a large dose of Italian individualism, account for the varied styles of Chianti Classico. According to government regulation there are two categories of Chianti. *Normale* is a much superior version of the wine that used to come in straw-encased, round bellied flasks (which are making something of a comeback). Aged for about a year, it is youthful, fruity wine and good company at daily meals. Chianti Classico *riserva* is made from a selection of the best grapes and aged for at least three years, usually in large oak casks. The finest riservas are full bodied wines of character that age with grace.

For over two decades a new category of red wine has been produced in Chianti. By law these wines, nicknamed Supertuscans by American admirers, have to be labelled *vino da tavola*, table wine, because the standard Chianti formula is totally set aside in their production. Some of these Supertuscans are pure Sangiovese, made from a clone of that grape called Sangioveto in certain parts of Chianti to distinguish it from its more common cousins. Some are combinations of Cabernet Sauvignon and other international red varieties with a Sangioveto base. Most are aged in small French oak casks. Many have been judged internationally to be among the best wines made in the world today, deep, rich, powerful and, using the ultimate adjective from my limited wine vocabulary, delicious.

One bottle or another of Chianti from the Classico area has been my house wine since my arrival in Tuscany fifteen years ago. I am not only a *chiantigiano* but also a *Gaiolese*, since I am a resident of Gaiole in

Chianti, one of the three ancient communes of medieval Chianti. During this period I have lived on three wine estates. Each of these family-owned vineyards, so different in dimension and spirit, typifies the developments in Tuscan wine making today.

My first home in Chianti was Riecine, a restored farmhouse and small vineyard, about five acres, in the hills above Gaiole. It is owned by John Dunkley, an Englishman who opted for early retirement from his advertising business in London and came to live in Chianti with his Italian wife, Palmina Abbagnano. I am their grandson's Godfather. They had invited me to spend the winter while I got the lay of the land and they took a well-earned holiday.

John and Palmina taught themselves the basics of wine-making, learning by trial and error and from the advice of experts and a little help from more experienced neighbours. They planted new vineyards, built a little cellar under the house, put in a swimming pool ('all work and no play . . .'), survived a couple disappointing vintages and the year I arrived had just received a gold medal, the first of many, for their 1975 *riserva*. There is not much to do on a small wine estate during the winter except to cut wood to keep the home fires burning. I also labelled several hundred bottles of the 1978 *riserva*, which earned me the right to drink a few. I forget the ratio.

Today, Riecine produces 15,000 bottles of Chianti Classico, about 3,000 bottles of a Sangioveto-based table wine called *La Gioia di Riecine*, as well as a couple thousand bottles of white. Over two decades of intelligent dedication, hard work and much pleasure have resulted in elegant wines of notable distinction.

In many ways the Dunkleys and Riecine are

outstanding micro-representatives of the contribution to the centuries-old tradition of wine-making made by foreigners, including non-Tuscan Italians, who bought mostly neglected properties in Chianti during the 1970s. They have brought to the area the newcomers' enthusiasm and energy. Considerable capital, as well as leisure time, has enabled them to concentrate on quality. They are savy about the international market-place and their presence has attracted the attention of the foreign press to the region's wine.

Just up the hill from Riecine is Badia a Coltibuono, one of the oldest and most prestigious wine estates in Tuscany, where I subsequently lived and worked for five years as director of promotions and public relations, a fancy title for what was a factotum job. Whereas Riecine, originally a *podere*, or tenant farm, on the once-immense Badia estate, must be one of the smaller Classico vineyards, Coltibuono is the largest family-owned and operated wine producer in the area. On 144 acres of prime vineyards planted on slopes carefully selected from the 2,000-acre property, Coltibuono produces 300,000 bottles of wine from estate-grown grapes and 500,000 bottles from grapes bought from other vineyards.

The estate has been owned by the family of Piero Stucchi-Prinetti since the early nineteenth century. Piero, half Florentine aristocrat and half Milanese business executive (a felicitous combination, as it turned out, for Coltibuono) took over the estate from his mother in the late 1940s and managed it, mostly from Milan, with tenacious dedication. The quality of the products, his marketing skills and business acumen brought Coltibuono through the difficult decades after the Second World War not only intact but also prospering, a small miracle that earned him the admiration and respect of his colleagues and not a little typical Tuscan envy.

Now two of Piero's children work full time for the family business. His daughter, Emanuela Stucchi, looks after marketing, promotions and public relations, and his son, Roberto, is in charge of production. Roberto is the first winemaker in the family and one of the first members of an Italian wine family to graduate from the renowned faculty of oenology and viticulture of the University of California at Davis.

Roberto and consultant oenologist, Maurizio Castelli, have been collaborating on the production of a line of wines for Coltibuono that includes exemplary traditional vintages, as well as innovations. They both are firm believers in the capacity for greatness of the Sangioveto grape, especially the clone that grows in Coltibuono's vineyards, which are among the oldest in Chianti, and concentrate much of their effort in bringing this noble variety to its full potential in the estate's *riserva*, which has remarkable ageing capacity, and in its *vino da tavola*, simply called *Sangioveto*.

San Giusto a Rentennano, where I reside now, at the southernmost part of the commune of Gaiole and the Classico zone, is a world apart. Viewed from the

Grape picking on the estate of San Giusto a Rentennano in Monti in Chianti.

exterior it is an idyllic, old-fashioned Tuscan estate. At its centre stands a gracious fifteenth-century villa with a lovely, crumbling stucco façade. The villa, enclosed by medieval walls with battlements, is surrounded by over six hundred acres of olive groves, vineyards, parcels of pasture land and cultivated fields and a few stone farmhouses scattered about. Within the vineyard buildings, however, and especially in the vats stored in the ancient cellar, new and exciting things are happening.

San Giusto is an estate in transition. Located at a strategic point on the ancient boundary between Florence and Siena, it was in the Middle Ages, a fortification of the Ricasoli family of Brolio castle, which still dominates from the hills above the estate. The Ricasoli installed nuns within its walls, presumably to pray for their protectors and to put the fear of God into their adversaries. It still belongs to a branch of that family, the Martini di Cigala, and has recently passed to a new generation of nine children.

Two brothers, Francesco and Luca, manage the estate. Francesco, ruddy, burly and bearded, is the winemaker. Until 1981, San Giusto sold its wine in bulk to large merchant houses, as well as to clients who came from near and far to fill their demi-johns.

When I arrived in Chianti, San Giusto was the last of the prestigious old estates where you could still purchase wine this way.

I remember taking an American wine merchant to San Giusto for a tasting shortly after they had begun bottling. His verdict: 'rustic but promising'. A few years later, one of the most respected wine critics in America wrote that their 1985 Classico was 'a wine with as much character and personality as a Chianti can obtain', and their 1985 *Percarlo*, a 100 per cent Sangioveto *vino da tavola*, 'a beautifully concentrated long, deep wine (that) rivals virtually anything ever produced in Italy'. Francesco, who is practically single-handedly responsible for this development, learned his art by osmosis and thanks to the discerning palate that also accounts for his reputation as an excellent cook.

Recently, Luca, dark, lean and intense, has joined his brother. He drives the tractor and tends the vines. As a viticulturist in the Chianti Classico zone, Luca finds himself in the enviable and rare position of still possessing prime sites on the property where new vineyards can be planted. These will enable San Giusto to gradually increase its currently small, 50,000-bottle production, which is practically sold while still in the cask.

The Martini brothers are proud to be *agricoltori*, farming wine-makers, with both hands in every stage of production from the soil to the presentation of their wines at tastings. They consider this factor the best guarantee that their wine will remain *genuino*, genuine, unadulterated, a quality that pertains as much to spirit as to substance.

Hidden deep within the recesses of the San Giusto cellars, where even I, who live only a stone's throw

The Martini brothers of San Giusto, Luca, left, and Francesco, winemaker, right, meditate on the fruit of their labours.

Like so many stalactites in an
enchanted cave, bunches of Malvasia
and Trebbiano grapes hang to dry for
Coltibuono's Vin Santo.

away, cannot get to, are several thousand bottles of a precious golden nectar called Vin Santo. How it got the name 'holy wine' is variously explained, quite probably because it was deemed the wine most worthy of the Holy Eucharist. Even in secular use there is something sacramental, in the sense of a sacred symbol, about Vin Santo. Tuscans usually keep it in the family's best crystal decanter and pour it to celebrate the arrival of an unexpected guest.

Great devotion goes into making Vin Santo. Traditionally, the first grapes picked at harvest time are the white Malvasia and Trebbiano for Vin Santo. Only the healthiest, ripest bunches are selected. These are then laid out on straw mats in a well-ventilated room and left to dry until they attain the desired concentration of sugar. This will be a period lasting two months if the winemaker wants the wine to be semi-dry, and at least ten weeks to make it sweet. At Badia a Coltibuono a large portion of the grapes for Vin Santo are dried by hanging the bunches from the rafters of an attic, where they look like so many stalactites in an enchanted cave.

When the grapes have suitably 'raisined' and the mouldy ones eliminated (no noble rot in the vinification of this dessert wine), they are pressed and the musts put into *caratelli*, small barrels, usually of oak or chestnut. Some producers, like the Martini brothers, leave residue from a previous vintage, called a *'madre'*, in the barrel. This, they claim, adds depth to the wine's character. Others prefer to make Vin Santo without this bacteria.

The barrels, which are not quite filled to the top to allow for oxidation during fermentation, are sealed with cement and stored directly under a roof of the winery, where the wine will be subject to the seasonal changes of temperatures for a minimum of two years and sometimes as long as six or eight. In a unique wine-making process during which the warm weather activates fermentation and the cold slows it down, the wine mysteriously acquires its characteristic amber colour and complexities of aroma and taste.

Obviously, making Vin Santo is a costly process from beginning to end and accounts for only a tiny per cent of any vineyard's overall production. San Giusto, whose Vin Santo is considered among Tuscany's most authentic and finest, rations it out in half bottles only, 2,000 of them to spread the wealth. It is rich and sweet, tasting of butterscotch and nuts with overtones of vanilla and orange, balanced by an acidity that gives it finesse and a dry, firm finish.

It is a venerable Tuscan tradition to dip *cantuccini di Prato*, those small, finger-shaped, hard almond biscuits (cookies), into your glass of Vin Santo. Francesco Martini serves his with the cheese course. When I have the rare good fortune to get ahold of one of his half bottles, there is no way I want to taste a residue of biscuit (cookie) crumbs when I drain my glass of this precious liquid, so I prefer to enjoy it as a delicious dessert on its own.

Panello con Uva
BETTI BIANCHI'S GRAPE BREAD

When I first met Betti Bianchi she was the baker's daughter in Gaiole in Chianti. Now she is the baker. During harvest time she turns out this grape bread in large sheets and you buy it by weight. She uses bunches of Sangioveto, the noble red grape of Chianti. You can substitute with any sweet red table grape. This makes a delicious coffeecake.

Serves 8.
7 oz/200 g (heaped cup) raisins
2 oz/60 g fresh yeast
2 lb/1 kg (8 cups) plain (all-purpose) flour
7 oz/200 g (1 cup) sugar
2 oz/60 g (½ stick) unsalted butter
5 oz/150 g (1 cup) shelled walnuts
2 tsp/10 ml mixed ground spices (apple pie mix)
1 tbsp/15 ml aniseed
1 sprig fresh rosemary
2 bunches red grapes

Soak the raisins in 8 fl oz/250 ml (1 cup) water to cover for about 20 minutes, then squeeze out excess water. Dissolve the yeast in the soaking water, then mix in the flour. Knead then leave to rise for 15 minutes.

In a large bowl, combine the sugar, butter, 3½ oz/ 100 g (⅔ cup) of walnuts, spices, aniseed, rosemary and 1 bunch of grapes. Add the dough and knead well about 10 minutes until it becomes smooth and elastic.

Knock down (punch down) the dough and stretch it to fit a round 8 inch/2 cm baking pan. Sprinkle with the remaining pine nuts and grapes and leave to rise for 20 minutes. Bake in a preheated 350°F/180°C/Gas mark 4 oven for about 30 minutes, until just golden and sound hollow if tapped on the bottom. Cool on a wire rack.

Betti Bianchi's grape and nut bread.

Cantuccini di Prato

ALMOND BISCUITS (COOKIES)

This is how these biscuits (cookies) are made on the estate of Badia a Coltibuono and served with their fine Vin Santo. Pour glasses for your guests and invite them to dip the biscuits into the wine.

Makes 36.
2 whole eggs and 2 yolks
10 oz/300 g (2½ cups) plain (all-purpose) flour
6 oz/180 g (scant 1 cup) sugar
1½ tsp/7.5 ml (⅔ cup) baking powder
pinch of salt
4 oz/125 g blanched almonds, coarsely chopped
1 tbsp/15 ml unsalted butter for baking sheet
1 tbsp/15 ml grated orange rind (peel)
1 tbsp/15 ml milk

Lightly beat 2 whole eggs and 1 yolk together. Combine the flour, sugar, baking powder with the beaten eggs and salt. Mix until a soft dough is formed. Add the almonds and orange rind (peel) and knead until almonds are well distributed.

Divide dough into equal portions and on a lightly floured surface roll into long sausage shapes. Mix the remaining egg yolk with the ~~mix~~ *milk*. Brush the dough rolls with the mixture. Arrange the rolls on a lightly buttered and floured baking sheet. Bake in a preheated 350°F/180°C/Gas mark 4 oven for about 15 minutes.

Remove the baking sheet from the oven and while the rolls are still hot and soft, slice the rolls on the diagonal about ½-inch/1 cm wide. Using a palete knife (spatula), separate the slices so they do not touch. Return to the oven and bake for a further 5 minutes. Cool on a wire rack.

A FINALE OF WHITE TRUFFLES

When the grape leaves have shrivelled on the vines and the last mushrooms and chestnuts have disappeared from the market stalls, just when you think this cornucopia of autumnal plenty has given its all, there is a final surprise in store, a rare treat that nature has kept hidden under the earth. Its impressive Latin name is *Tuber Magnatum Pico*, the Great Pico Tuber (Signor Pico was the eighteenth-century botanist who first classified it) better known as the *tartufo bianco*, Italy's prestigious and precious white truffle.

Discovering it in Tuscany comes as a double surprise to many who erroneously associate the white truffle exclusively with the area around the Piedmontese city of Alba. As a matter of fact, it can be found in a dozen different places along the Italian peninsula from Piedmont in the north to the Molise in the south. In Tuscany there are five zones where the white truffle grows. The largest is the Crete Senesi, an extraordinary land that extends south of Siena for some 500 square kilometres to the Renaissance hilltop town of Pienza.

Entering the Crete you immediately get the feeling that something mysteriously primal takes shape under this soil. As far as one can see are vast expanses of undulating clay hills created millions of years ago from deposits left by the receding sea. In some areas erosion has moulded the clay into steep ochre furrows that run in rhythmic rows along the slopes. In others, series of bleached white protuberances of cracked clay swell out of the terrain creating a lunar landscape. It is understandable that *crete*, which means 'clay' is often mistranslated into English as 'craters'. More than anything the sight resembles, as someone once wrote, 'a solidified sea in storm'.

As you drive along the crest of the hills you feel as if you were on the edge of a desert. Only a solitary farmhouse or a single cypress tree atop a knoll can be seen in the distance. The first impression is of a barren, desolate land, yet in the spring shepherds graze flocks of sheep on the blue-green grass and in the autumn farmers sow the fields with seed. And at the base of the valleys, along the grassy banks of streams and irrigation channels lined with willows and poplars, beneath the humid, lime-rich, sandy soil grows the white truffle.

Notwithstanding all the gastronomic fame and glamour associated with its name, the truffle is really nothing more than an underground, parasitic mushroom that sucks the sap from the roots of these trees. It is an odd looking little fellow to boot. The *Tuber Magnatum Pico* is called white in contrast to its poorer and blander cousin, the black truffle (*Tuber melanosporum*), which looks very much like a warty piece of coal. It, too, is found in Tuscany but is most associated with neighbouring Umbria and, of course, France's Pèrigord. The colour of the white truffle actually varies from a yellowish-grey to brown. In size, it can range from the dimensions of a large hazelnut of about ⅓ ounce/10 grams to a small orange of 3½ ounces/100 grams. Prize-winning tubers have weighed in at five times that size. It can be smooth and round if the soil where it took form was soft and loose, or knotty and irregular in shape if it had to struggle for space. Inside, the beige-coloured meat is compact and finely veined.

The white truffle is considered supreme for its unique aroma and taste. There is something elemental even archetypal about the smell of truffles. Other aromas are referred back to it. I have often heard

Beneath the humid, lime-rich, sandy
soil of the Crete Senesi grows Italy's
prestigious and precious white truffle.

wine-tasting experts describe the bouquet of a maturing fine vintage as having the scent of truffles. The fragrance is penetrating, pungent, musky and in a positive sense, faintly decadent. It makes a powerful physical impact. In *Gastronomy of Italy*, Anna del Conte describes the taste of truffles as 'a perfect marriage between a clove of garlic and a piece of the best Parmesan'. I have to take her word for it, for when I eat truffles so intoxicating is their aroma that I find it practically impossible to distinguish between what I am tasting and what I am smelling. I am not complaining. In this case ignorance is truly bliss.

In Tuscany the season for white truffles begins in October and ends in December. Every year on the third weekend of November, when they are most plentiful and most potent, this little lump reigns at the medieval castle of San Giovanni d'Asso, an ancient town in the midst of the Crete Senesi, where a celebration is held in its honour. During these days, even before reaching the inner courtyard of this

massive fortification, you are practically assaulted on the ramparts by the smell of truffles. Inside, heaps of them are spread out on counters manned by *tartufai*, licensed truffle hunters and members of a regional consortium, who weigh and sell their precious nuggets.

Prices fluctuate according to the law of supply and demand. At the height of a good season a *Tuber Magnatum Pico* of the hundred-gram size will sell for over two million lire per kilo, before the middle-men get involved. These dealers are essential to the livelihood of the hunters. They find the import-export and fine food markets that have the means to purchase and distribute large quantities of this pricey and highly perishable commodity. In the crowd I recognize the faces of several restaurateurs who are trying to strike a bargain. In a fancy Florentine restaurant a 8000 lire plate of pasta with a generous portion of white truffles shaved on top will end-up costing close to 40,000 lire.

With this kind of money exchanging hands the atmosphere surrounding these *tartufai*, locals turned international businessmen a few weeks of the year, is pretty heady. I have since discovered that in the days preceding the fair the café below the castle provides more relaxed surroundings than the market-place for chatting with the hunters. It was there that I met Vasco, a young, part-time, third generation *tartufaio*, employed in a terracotta factory, who introduced me to Betti, his small brown and white part-Pomeranian mongrel, whose pedigree as a truffle hunter goes back further than her master's. She is worth her weight in truffles, as well. A trained, experienced truffle dog sells for many millions of lire.

In the past sows instead of dogs were used to snort

Prime exemplars of *Tuber Magnatum Pico*, white truffles, worth their weight in gold.

Truffle hunters start out in search of
the hidden treasure soon after dawn.

Trained and experienced truffle dogs are worth many millions of lire.

Today, however, when time is big money and a certain swiftness in tracking the scent counts, pigs are too cumbersome to lug around in the little Fiats hunters use to move from one truffle deposit to another. Piggy appetites also get in the way of work. Quite understandably, I think, they experience an almost uncontrollable urge to eat this delicacy once they have snouted it out, and it is difficult to convince them otherwise. German scientists have discovered that truffles contain a substance which gives off a musky aroma similar to the sexual hormone of the male pig, which provides a Freudian explanation for what all the excitement is about and maybe not just for lady pigs. There is an ancient, well-documented, popular belief that truffles are an aphrodisiac for humans as well.

Small, short-haired dogs are more agile in the dense undergrowth where white truffles grow, and can be trained to wait for an alternative food reward when they have caught the scent of truffles. In Betti's case this is a piece of pork sausage. Some hunters addict their dogs at the teat by rubbing the mother's nipples with a truffle. Vasco thinks this method makes them too keen. He began training Betti when she was three months old by teaching her to retrieve a small cloth ball with a bit of sausage inside. He later hid the sausage-ball under a few centimetres of earth for Betti to discover. Finally, he buried a piece of truffle to 2–8 inches/5–20 cm under the earth, the depth at which white truffles grow, and always rewarded Betti with a hefty piece of sausage when she found the spot.

Every morning before work soon after dawn (nocturnal hunting is illegal) Vasco takes Betti out in the open fields to a promising place and lets her loose. When she thinks she has scented a truffle deposit and

out the buried treasure. In the principal chamber of Siena's *Palazzo Pubblico*, a celebrated fourteenth-century fresco painted by Ambrogio Lorenzetti depicts the good life of an industrious Siena countryside. The scene takes place within the landscape of an austere and almost geometrically cultivated Crete Senesi. Prominant in the foreground, walking along the side of a road travelled by merchants with their goods on mules and Lords and Ladies mounted on horseback, is a man urging along his pig with a stick. They may be simply out for a stroll but my guess is that they are after truffles, which were beginning to make a comeback on the tables of the aristocracy in the late Middle Ages after an absence dating from the decline of the Roman Empire.

starts to dig, he coaxes her off quietly not to attract the attention of the competition, and carefully continues the digging himself with a *vanghetto*, a small spade on a solid short wooden handle. If Betti's senses have served her right, she gets her usual reward and, in accordance with Tuscan regional regulations, Vasco fills in the hole with the same soil he dug out so the truffle spores may reproduce.

During the three days of the San Giovanni d'Asso fair, gastronomic stands set up around the castle grounds feature truffle dishes. On the Sunday guest chefs create a five-course menu based entirely on white truffles. The meal, costing about 70,000 lire, is served at a single sitting in the basement of the town recreational centre. Several restaurants in the Crete Senesi follow suit.

White truffles are always eaten raw, shaved over food in flakes. The purpose is to feast on *them* and to shave away as generously as your finances permit. The dish they accompany is secondary. The food ought to be rich so it stands up to the aroma and taste of the truffle but uncomplicated so it doesn't distract from them. If the food is also warm, I find it intensifies these qualities all the more.

A typical menu at one of these festive white truffle banquets might be an *antipasto* of *crostini caldi alla crema di tartufi*, warm little toasts with a truffle cream; *insalata di tartufi e parmigiano*, a salad of truffles and thin slices of Parmesan dressed with lemon and olive oil; *taglierini ai tartufi*, long, thin home-made pasta dressed in butter and truffles; *scaloppine di vitello con tartufi*, veal scallops sautéed in red wine with truffles; and for dessert, not on the usual menu but a combination suggested by a chef friend from California at a meal when there was still a bit of truffle left to shave at the end: a slice of the darkest, richest, most decadent chocolate tart possible, whitened by a flurry of truffles.

White truffles are one of those things of which only too much is enough, an indulgence not many bank accounts allow. I have found, however, that the illusion can be created. For less than the price of one of those meals, I can bring home an ample ¾ oz/20 g nugget, fry a couple of eggs in butter and shave the truffle over the dish with abandon. This provides me with a taste of Tuscany I will recall all winter long.

Panini al Tartufo
ROLLS WITH TRUFFLE BUTTER

Truffle butter is a good way to make the taste of a little truffle go a long way. It can also be used to dress fresh egg pasta.

Makes 12.
12 small round dinner rolls or bridge rolls
4 oz/125 g (1 stick) unsalted butter, softened
1 tbsp/15 ml double (heavy) cream
salt and pepper
3 oz/90 g white truffle, finely grated

Tiny, glazed, oval rolls spread with truffle butter are a speciality of Procacci in Florence.

Warty, black summer truffles are milder in taste and more moderate in price than their white cousins.

Cut the rolls in half and remove the crumb from the lower half. Mash the butter in a small bowl, then add the cream and stir well. Season with salt and pepper. Add the grated truffle and stir well to blend.

Fill the lower halves of the rolls with the mixture, cover with the tops and serve chilled.

Sformato di Patate con Tartufi
— POTATO, HAM AND CHEESE LOAF WITH TRUFFLES —

White truffles are shaved over pasta, polenta and any number of other dishes rich enough to support their aroma and flavour but not so complicated as to overwhelm them. If you have truffles to spare, you can sprinkle some in between the layers of this loaf.

Serves 6.
1 lb/500 g potatoes
3½ oz/100 g (7 tbsp) unsalted butter
2 oz/60 g Parmesan cheese, grated
2 oz/60 g Emmenthal (Swiss) cheese, grated
salt and pepper
pinch grated nutmeg
1 egg, lightly beaten
5 oz/150 g cooked ham, sliced finely
7 oz/200 g mozzarella cheese, diced
2 tbsp/30 ml fine dry breadcrumbs
3½ oz/100 g white truffle

Boil the potatoes in their skins until tender, then peel and mash while still hot. Combine the mashed potato, 2 oz/60 g (½ stick) butter, the Parmesan and Emmenthal (Swiss) cheeses, salt, pepper, nutmeg and egg and mix until well blended.

Butter a small loaf (bread) pan. Using one-third of the potato mixture, make a layer in the pan. Cover with half the ham and mozzarella. Make another layer of potato and cover with ham and mozzarella. Top with the rest of the potato mixture, sprinkle with breadcrumbs and dot with the remaining butter. Transfer to a preheated 300°F/150°C/Gas mark 2 oven and bake about 20 minutes, until the cheese has melted. Remove the pan from the oven and let it rest for a couple of minutes, then turn the potato loaf onto a rectangular serving plate, sprinkle with shavings of truffle and serve immediately.

INDEX

Abbagnano, Palmina 144
acacia honey 80
acciughe (anchovies) 112-13
acquacotta 42, 45
affettato toscano 34-6
Agliana 72
agnello arrosto alla Romola 76
Aleatico (wine) 114
almond biscuits 29, 149
Anichini, Carlo 62, 64, 66
Anichini, Nella 62-6
Aniello, Michele 42
apis ligustica bees 78
arista al ramerino 118, 125-6
artichokes, sautéed 96
asparagini (wild asparagus) 50
asparagus omelette 60
aubergine, fried, and mixed vegetables
    seasoned with white wine vinegar 57

baccalà (salt dried cod) 108
baccalà alla fiorentina 108
bacon and eggs 138-40
Badia a Coltibuono 100, 145, 148
baked pasta mould with mozzarella and
    tomato sauce 105-6
ballocciori (boiled chestnuts) 134
ballotte (boiled chestnuts) 134
Barbara Guiffrida's edible weeds, wild
    greens, and flower salad 56
bean recipes 21, 60, 92, 126, 140-1
beekeeping 78-82
Betti Bianchi's grape bread 148-9
biscuit recipes 29, 149
black truffles 150
boar *see* wild boar
La Bottega del 30, Villa a Sesta
    (restaurant) 17-18, 19
bread:
    grape 148-9
    see also bruschetta; crostini; fettunta;
        panini
bresaola di cavallo (horse fillet) 42
broad beans, stewed 60

Brolio castle 102-5
bruciate (roasted chestnuts) 134
Brunello de Montalcino (wine) 8
bruschetta 18-20
bruschetta al cavolfiore 20
bruschetta al pomodoro 19
buccellato bread 130
buristo (blood sausage) 32, 34

cacciucco (fish dish) 108-10
cacciucco alla livornese 108
cake recipes 28-9, 141
caldarroste (roasted chestnuts) 134
Camelia, Franco 17-18
cantuccini di Prato 148, 149
capocollo (*coppa*) (pork cut) 33, 36
carciofi al tegame 96
Carmignano (wine) 58
Casella, Cesare 136-8
Casella, Pietro 136
Casella, Rosa 136
Casini, Luciano 111-14, 115
casserole recipes 45-6, 106-7
castagnaccio 134, 141
Castelli, Maurizio 145
castrabecco (wild salsify) 50
Catinari, Giannetto 72
Catinari, Roberto 72-4
cauliflower *bruschetta* 20
Cavriglia, snail *sagra* at 52, 119
cheese, sheep's milk 62-6
cheese recipes 69
chestnut blossom honey 80-2, 83
chestnut blossom honey ice cream 83
chestnut flour cake 141
chestnuts 132-5
Chianti casserole 106-7
Chianti Classico (wine) 8, 142-5, 146
Chianti *normale* (wine) 144
Chianti (wine) 142
Il Chiasso, Capoliveri
    (restaurant) 111-14
chick-pea soup, creamed, with
    croûtons 20-1

chicken liver toasts 123
Chini, Romola 75, 76
Chini, Vincenzo 30, 32-4
chocolate truffles 75
chocolates 72-5
Cibrèo, Florence 84, 87-90
ciccioli 84
cinghiale in agrodolce 38
cinghiale al seme di finocchio 42-4
Cioni, Carlo 58
colomba pasquale (sweet bread) 70-2
colombacci in galera 45-6
Coltibuono 100, 145, 148
coniglio ripieno arrosto 94-6
cookie recipes 29, 149
cooking classes 100-2
Corti, Giulio 90-1
courgettes marinated in olive oil with red
    wine vinegar 57
creamed chick-pea soup with croûtons
    20-1
creamed ricotta with raspberry purée 69
cremino di ricotta con lamponi 69
crescione dei prati (bittercress) 50
crostata di fragole 107
crostata di pere 97
crostini tradizionali 118, 123
cuffia tripe 86

Da Delfina, Artimino (restaurant) 58
Da Michele Ai Due Cippi, Saturnia
    (restaurant) 41-2
de'Medici, Lorenza 66, 100-2
Dolci & Dolcezze, Florence 90-2
duck, roast, with pomegranates 46
Dunkley, John 144

Easter 70-2
Easter eggs 72
eggplant, fried, and mixed vegetables
    seasoned with white wine vinegar 57
Elba 100-14

fagioli all'uccelletto 126

Festa dell'Unità 116
festa (festivals) 116-23
fettunta 17, 18-19
filetti di caccia (game meats) 42
finocchiona 34, 36
fish recipes 108-10, 114-15
Florence 84
Florentine meat and vegetable
    mixed-fry 61
frenacce (pancakes) 42
fresh tuna fish rolls 114-15
fried aubergine and mixed vegetables
    seasoned with white wine vinegar 57
frittata di asparagi 50, 60
frittata nera 32
fritto misto alla fiorentina 58, 61

gelato al miele di castagno 83
germano al melograno 44, 46
La Gioa di Riecine (wine) 144
gran farro della Garfagnana 140-1
guanciale (pig's cheek) 33

honey 80-2
honeydew 82
hunting 38-41

ice cream, chestnut blossom honey 83
insalata di funghi porcini 138
involtini di tonno 114-15
Italian trifle 123, 126

lamb, roast 76
lampredotto tripe 87
Lucca 130-2
Lucchesia 130-2, 134
Luciano's fish soup 115
lumaca (common land snail) 50-2
lumache al sugo 52

maialino arrosto 44
manna 82
Maremma area 39-42
Marrocchi, Anna 136

marroni chestnuts 132-4
Martini, Francesco 146, 148
Martini, Luca 146
marzolino cheese 62
Mascheroni, Carlo 53-4
meat and vegetable mixed-fry 61
melanzane e Giardiniera 57
mille fiori honey 82
minestrone con basilico e pinoli 94
Minucci, Miranda 66-8
misto alla Luciano 115
Montecristo 110
Monti dell'Uccellina 40
mushrooms 134-7

Nannini, Danilo 26
necci (chestnut flour pancakes) 134

octopus with potatoes 114
olio di frantoio 16
olive oil, 8, 16-17
olives 14-16
omelette, asparagus 60
ovolo (egg-mushroom) 136

Palio, at Siena 119-22
pan di ramerino buns 87
pancakes 42, 134
pancetta (pork belly) 33
panello con uva 148-9
panettone (christmas bread) 70
panforte (cake) 22-8
panforte Margherita 25-6
panini al tartufo 155-6
panpetato 25, 26, 28-9
pappa al pomodoro (soup) 118
pappardelle (noodles) 42, 118, 123
pappardelle with hare sauce 125
pappardelle sulla lepre 118, 125
Pasqualino (sausage) 34
passato di ceci con gli zoccoli 20-1
pasta recipes 18, 68-9, 83, 105-6
pear pie 97
pecorino cheese 62-6

pecorino romano 62
pecorino siciliano 62
pecorino toscano 62, 65
pepper cake 28-9
Percalo (wine) 146
Picchi, Benedetta 88-90, 92
Picchi, Fabio 84-90, 92
pie (fruit) recipes 97, 107
pig, family 30-4
pigeons 'imprisoned' in a covered
    casserole 45-6
polentine dolci 134
polpo con patate 114
Pontormo bacon and eggs 138-40
porcini mushrooms 135-6, 137
porcini salad 138
pork recipes 34-6, 37, 125-6
potato, ham and cheese loaf with
    truffles 156
Prato, Antonio 78-83
Prato, Christie 82
prosciutto toscano 33, 36

rabbit, roast, stuffed 94-6
raperonzolo (rampion) 50
raviggiolo cheese 64
ravioli con spinaci e ricotta 68-9
Ricasoli, Baron Bettino 102
Ricasoli, Baroness Costanza 102-3
ricciarelli alla mandorla 29
ricotta cheese 62, 66, 68-9, 83
Riecine 144-5
roast lion of pork 125-6
roast mallard duck with pomegranates 46
roast stuffed rabbit 94-6
rolls with truffle butter 155-6
Romola's roast lamb 76
rosticciana (pork ribs) 33
rucola selvatica (wild rocket) 50

sagre (food festivals) 52, 118-19
salad recipes 56, 138
salame toscano 34, 36
salsicce fresche 36

salsiccie toscane 36
salvastrella (salad burnet) 50
San Giovanni d'Asso 152, 155
San Giusto a Rentennano 145-6
Sangioveto (wine) 145
sanguinaccio (blood pudding) 32
Saturnia 41-3
sausages 34-6
schiacciate bread 87
sebadas (cheese snack) 66
sformati di fagiolini verdi e tonno 92
sformato di patate con tartufi 156
sheep's milk cheese 62-6
Siena 22, 119-22
sliced Tuscan pork meats 33, 34-6
snails 50-2
soppressata (brawn) 34, 36
soup recipes 20-1, 45, 94, 115, 140-1
spaghetti alla ricotta e miele 33
spaghetti del pastore 18
spaghetti with ricotta and honey sauce 83
spalla (pork shoulder) 33, 36
spiedini di maiale 37
spinach and ricotta ravioli with tomato
    sauce 68-9
spinach sautéed in olive oil 76
spinaci saltati 76
Stianti, Giovannella 53-4
Stoquelet, Hélène 17-18, 19
stracotto 106-7
strawberry tart 107
strigoli (bladder campion) 50
Stucchi, Emanuela 145
Stucchi, Roberto 145
Stucchi-Prinetti, Piero 66, 145
stufato di baccelli 60
Supertuscan wines 144

Taddeucci, Mario 130
tart (fruit) recipes 97, 107
tartufi fondenti alla Catinari 75
tartufo affogato (drowned truffle) 118
tartufo bianco (white truffle) 150-5
tegamata (sweetbreads) 32

terracrepolo (wall salad) 50
timballo con salsa di pomodoro 105-6
tomato *bruschetta* 19
tonno sott'olio (tuna in olive oil) 108
tortelli 42
trifle, Italian 126
trippa alla fiorentina 86
trippa (tripe) 84-7
truffle butter 155-6
truffles:
    black 150
    chocolate 75
    white 150-5
tuna, 92, 108, 112, 114-15
tuna and bean moulds 92
Tuscan bean and grain soup 140-1
Tuscan sausages 36
Tuscan skewered pork 37

uova e carne secca del Pontormo
    137, 138-40

vegetable soup with basil and
    pine nuts 94
vegetable soup with eggs 45
Vernaccia di San Gimignano (wine) 8
Vin Santo (wine) 148
vinegars 53-6
Vino Nobile di Montepulciano (wine) 8
Vipore (restaurant) 136-7
Vitali, Benedetta 84
Volpaia 53-6

white bean soup with olive oil 21
white beans and tomato 126
white truffles 150-5
wild boar:
    antipasto 42
    stewed 38, 41
wine vinegar 53-6

zuccini a scapece 57
zuppa alla frantoiana 21
zuppa Inglese 123, 126